Agentic AI and the Future of Work

How Intelligent Agents will redefine roles, skills, and value

Kieran Gilmurray

Copyright

Index

Agents are not only going to change how everyone interacts with computers. They are also going to upend the software industry, bringing about the biggest revolution in computing since we went from typing commands to tapping on icons. Agents won't simply make recommendations; they'll help you act on them.

Bill Gates on rise of AI Agents

Foreword

Across industries, one of the most in-demand AI technologies is Agentic AI. Everyone is talking about Agentic AI, but what is it, and how does it impact organizations like yours and individuals like you?

AI is changing industries at breakneck speed. But this is not the first-time technology that has disrupted organizations and jobs. When the internet or computers emerged, they redefined work. Nearly 70% of today's jobs did not exist 100 years ago.

With organizations racing to integrate AI and Generative AI into their organizations, Agentic AI, a subset of AI, is quickly becoming essential for shaping industry, roles, and organization AI.

Why this book and why now?

With 90% of US IT executives saying that business processes would improve by using Agentic AI, with 37% claiming they are using it, and with a further 32% planning to invest in it, there is no better time to learn about it than now.

Whilst many will claim that Agentic AI is a revolution in computing, I prefer to consider it an evolution. That said, this evolution of digital workers, agents, or agentic AI will have a much more dramatic impact on work and society than any AI we have seen to date.

Why?

Agentic AI does not just execute tasks. It thinks, plans, actions, and adapts. Agents can also collaborate with each other and people across computer systems and networks, reshaping and transforming how work gets done.

In many instances, AI agents will enhance workforce capabilities by autonomously problem-solving and completing complex tasks. For example, organizations that integrate autonomous agents effectively will unlock new levels of efficiency, agility, and intelligent decision-making, enabling them to scale operations without the traditional constraints of human resource capacity.

Yet increasingly, rather than assisting humans, as agents get smarter, they will increasingly replace human labor. Workers will need to focus on roles such as caregivers or those that involve AI technology, creative destruction, innovation, or other similar, non-AI, repeatable, high-value tasks to remain relevant. In the future, digital labor will become indispensable strategic assets, complementing and, many times, replacing human expertise to enable business owners to create new business models.

This is not a distant projection; industries are already being redefined by agents. As ever, the challenge for leaders is not just adopting these technologies but reimagining how organizations operate in a world where AI-driven systems can anticipate needs, negotiate deals, and create value independently of people, just like you and me. Agentic AI is not just yet another tech trend. Its impact on business will be profound.

AI agents will not just automate tasks but fundamentally reshape business models, supply chains, decision-making processes, and labor markets and models. Organizations that harness this shift will gain a strategic advantage, while those that hesitate may struggle to compete in an economy increasingly driven by intelligent automation.

This change has huge implications for workers, governments, educators, and workers everywhere.

Who should read this book?

Zero AI knowledge is needed to read this. This is a fantastic resource for managers, executives, consultants, and leaders looking to understand how to leverage AI for business growth and innovation. Business leaders, not just technologists, must understand how autonomous AI systems will redefine competitive advantage and global competitiveness.

Today's challenge is not just adopting AI but leading its implementation in ways that align with your future organization's goals and industry dynamics. And for that to happen you need to understand how to harness this hugely impactful technology before your competitors or new market entrants eat what is left of your lunch. This book is designed to help people just like you do just that.

What is in the book?

A book is needed to help you understand the impact of agent AI on organizations and workers everywhere to give you the knowledge you need to bridge the gap between technical innovation and executive strategy.

The book provides a collection of articles that combine into chapters to provide a comprehensive explanation of what Agentic AI is, how it functions and how it impacts your role and organization. It offers a deep dive into why organizations 'need' Agentic AI to stay competitive and efficient.

Additionally, it explores how to build and execute an effective Agentic AI strategy. The content includes numerous real-world examples of Agentic AI in action. Prioritizing Agentic AI leadership and adoption strategies, the book is designed to be accessible for business decision-makers.

Whether you are new to AI and Agentic AI or already have some knowledge, this book should be an invaluable resource for you.

Enjoy,

Kieran

Who is Kieran Gilmurray?

Kieran Gilmurray MBA (1st). MSc. PG Dip. Teaching, Directorship. Business Finance and Digital Marketing BSc. (Hons) Management Science

Kieran Gilmurray is an author, industry analyst, real-world business technology transformation strategist, and implementer. He is an internationally renowned AI, automation, data analytics and digital transformation expert. Kieran has over 30 years of experience developing innovative digital transformation solutions tailored to medium, large, and global-scale organizations.

He is known for his ability to provide actionable strategies that help organizations adapt and thrive in this digital world. Kieran's work has generated more than $300 million of value for organizations to date. His experience working with global enterprises in automation, AI, blockchain, data and cloud makes him a unique and highly sought-after consultant and advisor.

Kieran regularly delivers conference keynotes worldwide and appears on stage in front of some of the world's largest organizations. He is consistently ranked as one of the top global experts in Artificial Intelligence, Intelligent Automation, data analytics, brand influence and business technology innovation. He has received multiple international awards, including being named to prestigious lists such as the Top 50 Global Thought Leader and Influencer on Generative AI in 2025, the Top 50 Global Thought Leader and Influencer on Generative AI in 2024, a Best LinkedIn Influencer for AI and Marketing, Top 50 Global Thought Leaders and Influencers on Manufacturing 2024, Top 14 people to follow in data and one of the World's Top 200 Business and Technology Innovators.

His leadership roles for FTSE 100 organizations have focused on global artificial intelligence, intelligent automation, and technology business management, both as a strategist and an implementer. Kieran's expertise extends to building global intelligent automation centers of high and emerging technologies, significantly enhancing productivity, profitability, and overall business performance.

When he is not chairing international conferences or delivering masterclasses to industry leaders through organizations such as Emeritus or the prestigious Irish Management Institute (imi.ie), he is actively consulting for leading global organizations, driving AI, automation, digital transformation and innovation programs.

To stay updated on the latest trends in business technology, follow Kieran on his company's website: kierangilmurray.com or connect with him on LinkedIn, Spotify, YouTube, or X (formerly Twitter).

Kieran Gilmurray

CEO of Kieran Gilmurray and Company Limited a global technology consulting firm.

Introduction

How to Read this book.

I bet you already know how to read a book. You look at the cover; you examine the back. You might scan the chapter headings and glance at the opening paragraph. If it's a technical or business book, you may even look at the index.

Well, this book can be read sequentially, but you may see some core concepts crop up more than once, which is legitimate for the task at hand. As a result, you might be better served by dipping in and out.

That is because what you're holding in your hand is a manual designed to help the non-specialist line-of-business manager intrigued and inspired by all the current talk of Agentic AI. Someone who wants to see how they can start building an understanding before they use autonomous agents in their own organizations.

The guide is made up of a collection of articles covering a range of agentic AI concepts, best practices, and commonly used terms.

Agentic AI's benefits, which are real, do not come just from flicking a switch on a software robot or two in your accounts payable department. The reality is there is a big margin for error here. Wasted costs from poorly imaged or implemented digital transformation programs can be significant.

I authored this book to try and stop that from happening.

What I want to do, is to make it easier for people like you to make sense of agentic AI. Written to help clear some of the fog, it is the result of my own years of experience helping customers like you achieve long-lasting positive results with IT.

I hope that this book will help you and your organization become more successful using this wonderful technology however you choose to read it!

By Kieran Gilmurray

Intelligent Automation, Artificial Intelligence and Data Analytics Consultant Director

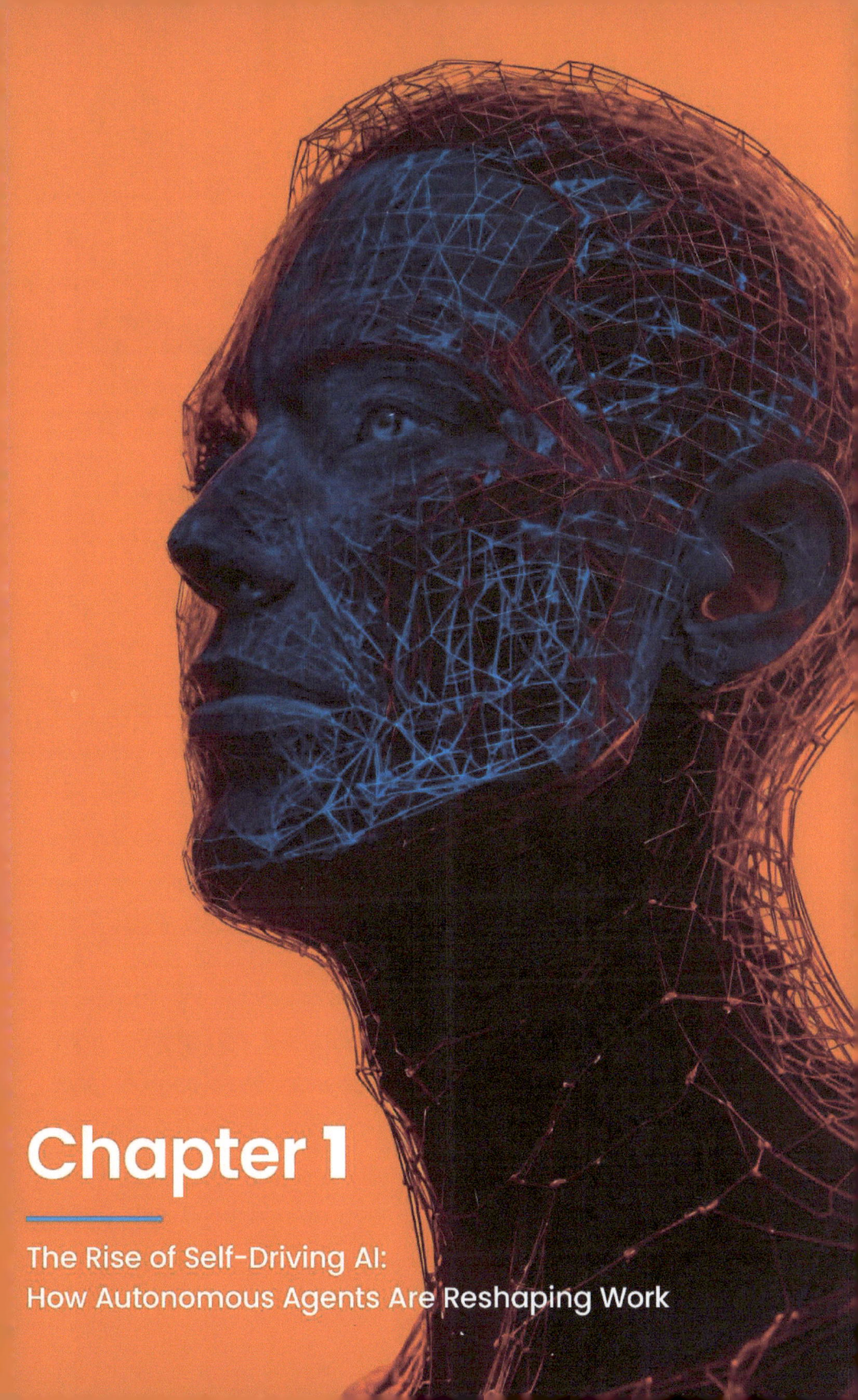

Chapter 1

The Rise of Self-Driving AI:
How Autonomous Agents Are Reshaping Work

The Rise of Self-Driving AI: How Autonomous Agents Are Reshaping Work

Picture this: a financial services firm deploys an AI agent that not only monitors market trends but also executes trades and mitigates risks in real-time. Meanwhile, a healthcare provider relies on AI agents to assist in diagnosing illnesses, recommending treatments, and scheduling follow-ups. These are not visions of a distant future, they are examples of how autonomous AI is revolutionizing the way we work today.

The evolution from assisted to autonomous AI marks a fundamental reimagining of how machines can work - from following human commands to independently solving complex problems. While traditional AI focuses on aiding human decision-making, autonomous agents are now capable of making decisions and taking actions independently. This transformation has profound implications for industries, organizations, and the workforce, ushering in an era of unprecedented efficiency and innovation.

The Evolution of AI Autonomy

From Rule-Based Systems to Adaptive Agents

AI's journey began with rudimentary systems designed to execute pre-defined rules. Early applications, such as chatbots and workflow automation, were limited by their reliance on static programming. However, breakthroughs in machine learning (ML) and reinforcement learning have paved the way for adaptive agents capable of analyzing data, learning from interactions, and autonomously solving complex problems.

Key Technological Breakthroughs

The emergence of large language models (LLMs) like Open AI GPTs, Google's Gemini, and Meta's Llama has been pivotal. These models enable natural language understanding and generation, allowing AI agents to comprehend instructions, process nuanced input, and deliver actionable insights. Combined with advancements in cloud computing, API integrations, and real-time data processing, LLMs have transformed AI agents into versatile tools for dynamic environments.

The Role of Large Language Models

LLMs serve as the cognitive engine of autonomous agents. Their ability to process vast datasets and contextualize information in human-like ways enables agents to reason, predict, and act with remarkable sophistication. For instance, LLM agents can streamline insurance claims, optimize supply chains, and personalize customer interactions, making them indispensable in modern enterprises. Their reach and use have accelerated as organizations learn to use them in more and more instances.

Industry Transformation

Every industry is being transformed by AI Agents. Let us take a sample of industries to highlight the impact agents are currently having on each.

Financial Services: Adaptive Trading and Risk Management

In financial services, autonomous AI agents are redefining trading and risk management. Unlike traditional AI tools, these agents analyze market data, adapt strategies, and execute trades without the need for human intervention. For example, organizations like Goldman Sachs are experimenting with AI agents capable of assessing market trends in real-time, autonomously optimizing portfolios based on shifting

13

conditions. These agents also enhance fraud detection by learning from patterns in transaction data, making them highly effective in identifying and mitigating fraud.

Healthcare: Proactive Patient Monitoring

Autonomous AI agents in healthcare are moving beyond diagnostics to deliver proactive care. Agents can integrate patient data from wearables and medical records, identify potential health risks, and even schedule follow-ups autonomously. For instance, AI-driven systems like Aidoc use imaging data to detect anomalies in radiology scans and recommend next steps to clinicians. This level of autonomy ensures faster diagnoses and improved patient outcomes.

Manufacturing: Autonomous Supply Chain Orchestration

In manufacturing, autonomous agents are taking supply chain management to the next level. These agents process data from IoT devices (Internet of Things), predict demand fluctuations, and autonomously adjust inventory and production schedules. For example, Siemens uses AI agents in smart factories to optimize workflows, monitor equipment health, and autonomously order supplies when needed. This minimizes downtime and ensures seamless operations, optimizing production expenses.

Customer Service: Hyper-Personalized Interactions

Autonomous AI agents are transforming customer service by delivering hyper-personalized experiences. AI agents go beyond responding to queries; they anticipate customer needs and provide tailored recommendations in real-time. A prime example is Amelia, an AI agent used by global enterprises to manage customer interactions autonomously. By learning from past interactions, Amelia continuously improves, offering a level of service that blends efficiency with empathy.

Impact on the Workforce

AI Agents will transform every role. Let us take a sample of roles to highlight the impact agents are likely to have on each.

Changing Job Roles

As autonomous AI takes over routine and decision-intensive tasks, job roles are evolving. Workers are transitioning from executors to strategists, focusing on areas where human creativity, empathy, and judgment are currently irreplaceable. This shift demands a redefinition of job descriptions and a re-evaluation of organizational structures.

New Skills Requirements

The rise of autonomous AI necessitates a workforce skilled in AI literacy, data analysis, and strategic thinking. Organizations must invest in reskilling and upskilling programs to prepare employees for this seismic transformation. Skills like problem-solving, adaptability, and ethical decision-making are becoming more critical than ever.

Human-AI Collaboration Models

Rather than replacing humans, autonomous AI is augmenting human capabilities. Collaborative models, where AI agents manage data-driven tasks while humans focus on oversight and strategic input, are becoming the norm. This symbiotic relationship enhances productivity and innovation across sectors.

Future Implications

Whilst industries and roles will change, this will not be without repercussions. The integration of autonomous AI with technologies such as the Internet of Things (IoT), quantum computing, generative AI, and edge computing is unlocking new possibilities. From smart cities to autonomous vehicles, these systems are poised to redefine industries and everyday life. Additionally, advancements in explainable AI are addressing concerns about a lack of transparency and trust.

The rise of autonomous AI brings ethical, legal, and societal challenges. Issues like bias in decision-making, data privacy, and the potential for job displacement require proactive solutions to protect workers and society. As such, organizations must establish frameworks to ensure responsible AI deployment to thrive in this new age of AI. For example, organizations should:

- Adopt a governance-first approach. Establish policies for ethical AI use and decision-making.

- Invest in workforce transformation. Provide training and resources to help employees adapt further to Agentic AI and every other change the Age of AI is bringing. This includes worker, leadership and manager training, both needed to manage and be managed by a combination of agents and human labor.

- Foster innovation. Encourage cross-functional collaboration to explore new AI-driven opportunities. In an age where continual technology-driven Schumpeterian disruption is a fact of life, the only way to remain relevant is to continually evolve.

- Organizations will never operate faster than they do today, nor will they ever operate slower. This requires a mindset and cultural change that few organizations are currently prepared for.

- Everyone must embrace an agile, data-driven, AI and digital-first mindset and operate without the traditional boundaries found within organizations. Innovation must come from everyone and in every direction if organizations are to succeed in the age of AI.

- Psychologically prepare an organization for cycles of shortened competitive advantage. Long gone are the days when executive teams, operating in predictable markets, set five- or ten-year strategies. Today, organizations must operate with far greater agility than at any point in their existence.

- Rather than one strategy, competitive advantage will now become a sequence of multiple smaller and shorter competitive strategies (think months, not years). Agentic labor will allow firms to build and destroy business models at lightning speed.

- Leaders must learn to deploy and destroy combinations or agentic and human labor at pace whenever and wherever opportunity exists.

Conclusion: Embracing the Future

The rise of autonomous AI marks a transformative moment in the evolution of work. By enabling machines to act with near-human cognition, this technology is reshaping industries, enhancing productivity, and redefining the role of humans in the workplace.

Organizations that embrace this shift with a forward-looking mindset will not only gain a competitive edge but also contribute to a future where technology and humanity work together to solve the world's most pressing challenges. The journey from assisted to autonomous AI is just beginning, and the possibilities are as vast as they are exciting.

This book looks at what is already happening now and helps articulate what is coming ahead to help you successfully navigate this exciting and disruptive time ahead.

Chapter 2

The Third Wave of AI:
Understanding the Rise of Agentic AI

2

The Third Wave of AI: Understanding the Rise of Agentic AI

The landscape of artificial intelligence (AI) has undergone significant transformation, evolving through three distinct waves.

The first wave, predictive AI, focused on analyzing historical data to forecast future trends to support data-driven decision -making. It enabled organizations to predict outcomes but lacked the capability for creativity or autonomous action. The second wave, generative AI, introduced the ability to create content, allowing systems to engage in human-like conversations, generate images, and produce written content. Generative AI captivated industries with its creativity and versatility but remained fundamentally reactive to human input.

Now, we stand on the cusp of the third wave: agentic AI. Unlike its predecessors, agentic AI represents a fundamental shift in capability. It enables AI systems to act autonomously, make decisions, and adapt dynamically to complex environments. This evolution is fuelled by the convergence of technologies such as advanced machine learning, cloud computing, and large language models (LLMs).

Together, these advancements empower AI systems to not only understand human intent but also to independently execute tasks and collaborate with other agents to achieve goals. As such, the age of agentic AI is not just about automation; it is about endowing machines with agency.

Decoding Agentic AI: A New Era of Autonomy

Agentic AI is characterized by its ability to operate independently, adapt to new situations, and continuously improve through self-learning. At its core, Agentic AI embodies three key traits:

- **Autonomous Decision-Making**: Unlike traditional systems, agentic AI can make decisions aligned with predefined objectives without requiring constant human oversight.

- **Adaptability and Self-Improvement**: Agentic systems learn from their interactions, refining their strategies and optimizing processes over time.

- **Goal-Oriented Behaviour**: Agentic AI focuses on achieving specific outcomes, breaking down complex tasks into manageable subtasks.

From Predictive AI to Generative AI to Agentic AI

To fully appreciate Agentic AI, it is essential to understand its evolution. Predictive AI provided actionable insights but was inherently static and limited to predefined scenarios. Generative AI broke new ground by enabling content creation and conversational interactions. Agentic AI, however, transcends both, allowing systems to execute actions, interact with multiple agents, and autonomously complete end-to-end processes.

Attribute	Agentic AI	Generative AI
Main Purpose	Autonomous action and decision-making	Content creation based on training data in response to user prompts
Autonomy	High; acts independently to set and pursue goals	Low; reacts to user input and cannot set its own goals
Adaptability	Can adjust its behavior in response to changing conditions of real-world or virtual environments	Shows some adaptability but cannot independently adapt to fully new or unstructured environments
Goal Setting	Capable of setting its own goals	No independent goal setting; operates within predefined constraints
Human Oversight	Minimal; able to function with little to no human intervention	Necessary; operates based on user-provided prompts
Learning Ability	Can continuously learn from interactions and update its decision-making process	Limited to its training data; does not learn dynamically in real-time
Interaction Style	Operates proactively and can initiate actions	Responds reactively to user prompts
Complex Task Execution	Can plan and execute multi-step tasks autonomously	Generates outputs based on isolated prompts, without independent task management
Use Cases	Autonomous agents, robotics, AI-driven decision-making systems	Text/image/video generation, chatbots, creative assistance

Agentic AI versus Generative AI

The Role of LLMs in Agentic AI

Large language models, such as GPT-4, serve as the "brains" of Agentic AI. They enable systems to understand nuanced human instructions, reason through complex scenarios, and make decisions based on context. By integrating advanced natural language processing capabilities, LLMs ensure that Agentic AI can seamlessly interpret and act on user intent. This capability transforms AI from a passive assistant into an active collaborator.

Enabling Infrastructure: Enterprise Integration

The rise of Agentic AI is also supported by robust enterprise infrastructure. Cloud computing provides the scalability needed to process vast amounts of data, while integration with existing business systems ensures seamless workflows. Data accessibility and interoperability further enhance Agentic AI's ability to deliver actionable insights and optimize operations in real-time.

Key Technology Trends: The Path Forward

Agentic AI is propelled by several technological trends that define its future trajectory.

Multi-Agent Systems

The orchestration of multiple agents is a hallmark of Agentic AI. These systems rely on sophisticated communication protocols and coordination strategies to achieve scalability and efficiency. By leveraging multi-agent collaboration, organizations can tackle complex tasks that exceed the capabilities of individual agents.

Enterprise Integration

The seamless integration of Agentic AI with existing systems is essential for success. APIs and secure data pipelines enable smooth interactions between AI agents and enterprise tools, ensuring efficient data flow and enhanced performance monitoring.

Future Developments

Emerging capabilities, such as advanced reasoning, emotional intelligence, and proactive problem-solving, will further expand the horizons of Agentic AI. Ongoing research and innovation promise breakthroughs that will continue to redefine the boundaries of what AI can achieve.

Business Opportunities: Unlocking Potential

Agentic AI presents transformative opportunities across industries, enabling organizations to redefine workflows and achieve unprecedented efficiencies. One of its most significant contributions is the automation of end-to-end workflows. By dynamically adapting to changing conditions, these systems streamline processes, reduce manual intervention, and minimize errors across a whole range of business areas. For example, in logistics, Agentic AI can optimize delivery routes in real-time, factoring in traffic, weather, and demand fluctuations.

Yet, the true power of Agentic AI lies in its ability to coordinate multiple agents. These agents specialize in different tasks, working together in a division of labor that mirrors human collaboration. For instance, in customer service, one agent might resolve a billing issue while another addresses technical support. Such ecosystems of collaborating agents enhance efficiency and enable organizations to scale operations effortlessly.

Industry Applications

With its ability to reason, coordinate and act, Agentic AI is already making waves in a wide variety of sectors. For example,

- **Healthcare**: Automating patient care plans, optimizing resource allocation, and providing real-time diagnostics.

- **Finance**: Enhancing risk assessment, fraud detection, and portfolio management through continuous data analysis.

- **Customer Service**: Managing complex support queries autonomously, reducing response times, and improving customer satisfaction.

- **Supply Chain**: Offering dynamic optimization and planning, ensuring agility in fluctuating market conditions.

Risks and Challenges: Navigating the Complexities

Whilst Agentic AI promises transformative benefits, it also introduces significant challenges that organizations must address if they are to responsibly leverage its full benefits.

Trust and Transparency

A key concern is ensuring that autonomous systems make decisions transparently. Organizations must implement explainable AI frameworks to provide users with insights into how decisions are made. Building trust requires systems to demonstrate reliability and maintain accountability, especially in high-stakes scenarios such as healthcare or finance.

Workforce Impact

The adoption of Agentic AI raises concerns about job displacement. However, it also creates opportunities for new roles, such as agentic AI trainers and workflow designers or orchestrators. The workforce of the future will require reskilling, with an emphasis on collaboration between humans and AI. Employees must learn to delegate effectively and manage AI agents to maximize their potential.

Ethical and Regulatory Considerations

The deployment of Agentic AI must adhere to strict ethical and regulatory standards. Issues such as data privacy, accountability for AI decisions, and compliance with governance frameworks will be critical to mitigating risks and ensuring responsible AI adoption.

Conclusion: Embracing the Agentic AI Era

The third wave of AI, Agentic AI, ushers in a new era of possibilities, where machines can autonomously execute tasks, collaborate with other agents, and adapt to dynamic environments. While the opportunities are immense, so are the challenges. Organizations must navigate the complexities of trust, workforce transformation, and ethical deployment to fully realize the potential of Agentic AI.

The time to prepare for this transformation is now. By embracing responsible adoption and fostering collaboration between humans and AI, organizations can harness the power of Agentic AI to drive innovation, efficiency, and growth. The future of work is here, and it is powered by Agents.

References

- https://www.pwc.com/m1/en/publications/documents/2024/agentic-ai-the-new-frontier-in-genai-an-executive-playbook.pdf

- https://www.uipath.com/ai/agentic-ai

- https://blogs.nvidia.com/blog/what-is-agentic-ai/

- https://www.endava.com/glossary/agentic-ai

Chapter 3

Agentic AI Mapping
the Road to Autonomy

CHAPTER **3**

Agentic AI Mapping the Road to Autonomy

Imagine you have just wrapped up a brainstorming session brimming with fresh ideas, and now your phone pings with urgent notifications, each pulling you in a different direction. Your project timeline is evolving by the minute, and routine tasks are piling up. It can feel like you are sprinting on an endless treadmill. Here's where agentic AI steps in to transform how we work: not just by automating tasks but by growing into an autonomous problem-solver that adapts to shifting demands.

Think of it as a step-by-step journey. At first, AI might help you filter email or schedule a few meetings, like a helpful (but limited) digital assistant. Over time, these systems learn to connect the dots across workflows, spotting inefficiencies and proposing solutions without waiting for explicit prompts. Eventually, they mature into self-updating, strategic partners who are capable of analyzing your organization's goals, refining their own processes, and autonomously deciding the best route forward.

This roadmap from basic automation to dynamic, self-improving agents is not just for tech gurus or C-suite executives; it is a blueprint for anyone curious about how AI can shoulder the busywork and free us to focus on what matters most.

By understanding each stage, from simple task augmentation to fully autonomous knowledge work, we empower ourselves to harness AI's potential responsibly, ensuring that these digital collaborators work alongside us as creative, adaptable teammates rather than mere tools.

Defining Agentic Automation
Bridging the Gap Between Automation and True Autonomy

Let us pause for a moment on the term "agentic automation." You have probably heard a lot about AI and automation and maybe even used chatbots that answer basic questions or software that scans invoices. While these tools do speed things up, most still work off rigid instructions. Think of it like an assembly line: fast but stuck following the same loop, day in and day out.

Agentic AI breaks free from that loop. It shifts from simple, rules-based "do this exactly" tasks to dynamic, "figure out the best way to do this" decision-making. Picture a chatbot that not only recognizes a frustrated customer but also adapts its responses to defuse tension, escalating to a human representative if needed. That extra context and adaptability is where traditional automation ends and agentic AI begins.

Why "Levels" of Agentic Automation? Understanding the Journey from Helper to Autonomous Partner

Just like there is a difference between a car's basic cruise control and a self-driving vehicle, AI solutions are not all created equal. Some are incredibly good at one or two tasks, while others can strategize, pivot, and even learn from mistakes. That is why we talk about "levels" of agentic AI: it gives everyone, from curious newcomers to seasoned tech leaders, a shared framework for assessing how advanced a system really is.

These levels hinge on three key ideas: reasoning, collaboration, and action. At lower levels, the AI might be helpful in a narrow capacity, like suggesting product recommendations or summarizing an email. At higher levels, it can chain tasks together, plan ahead, and adapt as it goes, edging closer to genuine autonomy.

By mapping these levels, teams can avoid overhyping what AI can do and focus on rolling out capabilities that match their readiness, data quality, and ethical standards. Each rung of the ladder offers new opportunities to streamline work, but it also brings fresh questions about security and oversight. If we navigate this path wisely, we can fully tap into AI's transformative power without losing sight of the human values that should guide it.

Below is a schematic outlining the five levels of agentic automation:

Level	Capabilities	Examples	Human Oversight	Challenges
Level 1: Simple AI Augmentation	Performs single-step tasks, provides recommendations, and highlights relevant information.	Email auto-sorting, grammar correction, sentiment analysis.	High: AI suggests actions but does not execute.	Limited adaptability and struggles with unexpected inputs.
Level 2: Task-Specific Agentic Assistants	Manages multi-step tasks, integrates information from multiple sources, requires human approval.	AI-powered scheduling, personalized sales outreach, automated report generation.	Moderate: AI executes but requires human approval.	Requires clean data and clear approval workflows.

Level 3: Self-Guided Execution & Reflection	Evaluates its own work, adjusts plans based on feedback, and manages more complex workflows.	Project management AI that adjusts deadlines and financial reconciliation with proactive adjustments.	Lower: AI self-corrects but still escalates complex issues.	Needs guardrails to prevent errors and requires strong data monitoring.
Level 4: Adaptive, Self-Updating Agents	Learns and adapts dynamically, updates its own strategies, and optimizes processes in real-time.	Supply chain AI that adapts procurement strategies, marketing AI that optimizes campaigns on the fly.	Minimal: AI adjusts its own processes but follows predefined ethical boundaries.	Complex governance and oversight, ensuring ethical AI decision-making.
Level 5: Fully Autonomous Digital Worker	Works independently across domains, sets its own goals, and makes decisions without human oversight.	Theoretical AI capable of research, negotiation, and strategic decision-making without prompts.	None: AI operates autonomously, requiring only high-level supervision.	Ethical risks, accountability concerns, and lack of real-world implementation.

The 5 levels of agentic automation

Level 1: Simple AI Augmentation: Laying the Foundation for Smarter Workflows

At Level 1 automation, AI is more of a helpful assistant than a bold decision-maker. It might tidy up your inbox, highlight crucial data points, or spot early warning signs of fraud. In other words, it handles single-step tasks, no multi-phase planning, and no detours if something unexpected pops up.

You will see tools that auto-complete text, flag emotions in customer feedback, or sift through resumes for certain keywords. They do not overhaul entire workflows, but they shave off the little annoyances that eat away at your day.

Picture a document-editing AI that suggests better word choices and flags inconsistencies. It is not booking follow-up meetings or looping in your project management tool yet, but it is already saving you from the tedious back-and-forth of manual proofreading. Or maybe you have a hiring platform that suggests the top applicants based on the job description. It will not negotiate salaries or schedule final interviews, but it certainly streamlines the early screening process.

Organizational Advantages and Risks

What do you get out of Level 1? Immediate wins. Repetitive chores become faster and more accurate, leaving you free to focus on deeper, more creative tasks. Meanwhile, your team starts getting comfortable with AI as a regular part of the workflow, an essential stepping-stone before adopting anything more advanced.

Of course, it is not all smooth sailing. Because these systems work off predefined patterns, they can stumble when faced with genuinely novel questions or data they were not trained on. They also require consistent human guidance to ensure quality. Still, Level 1 is a sweet spot for many organizations: it is easy to deploy, delivers quick results, and serves as a testing ground for the bigger leaps in autonomy still to come.

Level 2: Task-Specific Agentic Assistants: From Single-Step Helpers to Multi-Step Partners

Picture yourself delegating a task like writing follow-up emails, pulling customer data, and scheduling key meetings, all with one simple request. That is the magic of Level 2 AI. While Level 1 systems shine at single-step chores (think auto-completes or basic text suggestions), Level 2 task-specific assistants go a step further: they weave multiple actions together without constant human nudging.

Instead of just recommending an email subject line, a Level 2 agent can craft a personalized note, find the best time on your calendar, and send the message, automatically queuing follow-ups if there is no reply. It is about chaining tasks, not just tackling them in isolation.

You might see this in a sales context: the AI combs through your CRM to see past interactions, whips up an outreach plan, and schedules calls according to the customer's time zone. While a person might give a final thumbs-up, they are no longer babysitting each step.

Considerations

The real payoff here is the freed-up mental bandwidth. You offload bigger chunks of routine work so you can focus on brainstorming new product ideas or fine-tuning your strategy. But keep in mind that Level 2 AIs are still bound by the data and parameters you set. When they veer off track, maybe they cannot find a file or run into a new scenario, and they'll ping you to get back on course.

To get the most out of these AI assistants, businesses need to ensure their data is well-organized and easy to access. This means having clear records, structured databases, and tools that allow AI to pull the right information when needed, much like a well-maintained customer relationship management (CRM) system or an easy way for different software to share data. It is also important to set clear rules about how much independence the AI should have. Should it just suggest actions, or can it take steps on its own? Defining these boundaries ensures AI helps the business without making decisions outside its role.

Essentially, Level 2 is the sweet spot for many teams: enough automation to deliver serious efficiency gains but still grounded by human oversight to catch mistakes before they become headaches.

Level 3: Self-Guided Execution & Reflection: When AI Learns to Check Its Own Work

Now imagine an AI agent that does not just follow a script but actively stops to ask: "Is my approach working?" that is Level 3. It is where the system gains an internal "feedback loop" to evaluate each step, fine-tuning its tactics or backtracking if something looks off.

Richer Planning

At this level, AI starts to feel more like a collaborator than a tool. It can juggle multi-department workflows, keep an eye on progress, and pivot if data or circumstances change. Maybe it is performing a complex financial reconciliation: comparing records across multiple platforms, spotting a discrepancy, and automatically digging deeper to resolve it and only escalating to you if the problem gets truly sticky.

Think of a project management agent tasked with rolling out a new software update. After building a timeline, it notices that a key developer is overbooked. Rather than waiting for you, it proactively shifts deadlines, reassigns tasks, or flags bottlenecks to the team. The result? Fewer last-minute scrambles and a system that actively prevents chaos instead of just reacting to it.

Governance and Safety Nets

While Level 3 agents manage surprises better than their predecessors, they're not infallible. You still need well-defined guardrails, like a legal team reviewing certain updates or a manager verifying major changes. From a tech standpoint, all that active monitoring and reflection calls for strong data orchestration, logging, and version control so you can trace every decision the AI makes.

By spotting roadblocks and adjusting course before you even realize there is a problem, Level 3 agents free you to focus on high-level strategy, confident that the details are under control.

Level 4: Adaptive, Self-Updating Agents: When AI Learns, Evolves, and Optimizes on the Fly

Now, picture an AI agent that not only organizes tasks but also rewrites its own rulebook when it spots a better way to achieve results. That is Level 4. It is all about constant adaptation as well as growing smarter as new data, tools, and challenges come into play.

Unlike previous levels, these AI systems do not just follow a plan or tweak small details. They are empowered to rework their entire approach if it leads to a more efficient outcome. For example, an adaptive supply chain agent might notice that a new shipping route saves time and money, so it updates its logistics processes on the go.

Consider a marketing AI that detects sudden changes in audience behaviour maybe a spike in certain time zones or a shift in buyer demographics. Instead of waiting for someone to program a new strategy, it adjusts the entire campaign automatically: changes ad placements, alters messaging, and even refines budget allocations to fit the new reality. All you do is set the guardrails, like budget limits or brand guidelines, and let the AI drive.

Key Challenges

Giving AI this level of freedom raises the stakes. You want it to learn but not to run wild, especially in sensitive areas like finance or healthcare. That means setting strict "rules of the road" with oversight mechanisms that alert you if something goes off course. Also, because these agents can rewrite parts of their own operating procedures, the technical underpinnings are more complex. You will need robust logging, versioning, and ethical guidelines so that when your AI updates itself, it is always with your organization's values and goals in mind.

The Payoff: You gain a tireless partner that evolves alongside shifting market conditions, data flows, or user feedback. Level 4 agents manage complexity with agility, letting humans stay focused on creative problem-solving and big-picture vision, freeing you from routine course corrections and outdated workflows.

Level 5: The Fully Autonomous Digital Worker: A Glimpse into Tomorrow's Uncharted Frontier

This is where AI starts to sound almost science fiction: a fully autonomous digital worker capable of near-human adaptability across any domain, no prompts needed, no scripts required.

While we are not quite there yet, envisioning Level 5 offers a peek at just how transformative agentic AI could become.

Imagine an agent that does not just carry out tasks independently but actively sets its own tasks based on high-level goals. It could propose new research directions, negotiate deals in emerging markets, or dream up marketing campaigns without a single prompt, all while cross-checking data and learning from experience.

From a speculative standpoint, this raises intriguing (and sometimes unsettling) questions. Could an AI at Level 5 propose entirely new research directions for a pharmaceutical company or negotiate business deals in emerging markets? Might it devise creative advertising campaigns based on cultural cues it is gleaned from live data feeds all without a human stepping in to set guardrails? Advocates argue that such an agent would free humans from administrative drudgery, ushering in an era where we focus on creativity, strategy, and moral judgment. Critics counter that handing over so much autonomy to AI could erode essential human roles or create new risks that we are ill-prepared to handle.

This naturally leads to philosophical debates about personhood, consciousness, and moral responsibility. While it is doubtful that even the most sophisticated AI would magically become "self-aware," the mere possibility of an entity with open-ended learning and near-limitless computational power forces us to grapple with issues of control, accountability, and shared values. Even if it can manage unforeseen tasks, should a Level 5 agent be allowed to act freely in high-stakes scenarios, like healthcare diagnostics or government policy advice?

From a technical viewpoint, achieving true Level 5 autonomy would involve breakthroughs that rival or surpass current state-of-the-art AI research. New models of reasoning (beyond LLMs and reinforcement learning), better ways to manage uncertainty, and extremely robust safety mechanisms would be prerequisites.

Given the complexity, it is possible we will not see production-grade Level 5 systems for many years, if ever. Even so, imagining this theoretical endpoint helps us understand the trajectory of agentic AI. By thinking through the best- and worst-case scenarios now, we can start building ethical frameworks, regulatory measures, and cultural readiness to ensure that, if (and when) Level 5 does arrive, it serves humanity's broader interests rather than undermining them.

Conclusion: A Smarter Partnership Between Humans and AI

The rise of agentic AI is not just about building smarter machines. It is about reshaping how we work, think, and collaborate. From simple AI-powered assistants that lighten our daily workload to adaptive, self-improving agents that refine their own strategies, the road to autonomy is unfolding step by step. And while full-fledged digital workers may still be on the horizon, we are already seeing how AI can transition from a helpful tool into a true partner.

What is clear is that each level of agentic AI unlocks new opportunities but also raises new challenges. Level 1 and 2 agents boost efficiency and take care of routine tasks, freeing up time for deeper, more creative work. Level 3 introduces self-guided execution, allowing AI to plan, adjust, and learn from its own mistakes. By Level 4, AI is not just following instructions, it is reworking its own processes to optimize outcomes in real-time. At the theoretical Level 5, AI reaches the frontier of fully autonomous digital knowledge work, opening both incredible possibilities and weighty ethical questions.

But no matter how advanced AI becomes, one thing remains constant: the need for human oversight, creativity, and strategic thinking. The best AI systems do not replace us, they amplify our strengths, helping us focus on the things that truly matter. The key is to strike the right balance: embracing AI's capabilities while ensuring that its development remains aligned with human values, ethical principles, and responsible governance.

Agentic AI is not just about automation. It is about transformation. It is about reclaiming time, enhancing decision-making, and working alongside intelligent systems that can navigate complexity with us. As we step into this new era, the real power of AI lies not in replacing human ingenuity but in unlocking its full potential.

References:

- https://blogs.nvidia.com/blog/what-is-agentic-ai/

- https://outshift.cisco.com/blog/agentic-AI-intelligence-for-enterprise-use

- https://hai.stanford.edu/news/human-centered-approach-ai-revolution

Chapter 4

Effective AI Agents –
Best Practices and Future Directions

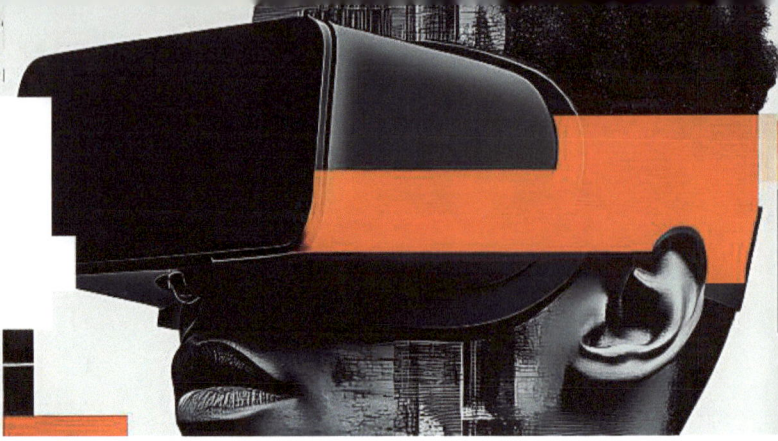

Effective AI Agents - Best Practices and Future Directions

AI agents have evolved dramatically over the past number of decades. From early symbolic AI systems, like the General Problem Solver, to today's sophisticated generative AI models, their journey shows humanity's relentless pursuit of automation and intelligence. Yet, even as LLMs demonstrate an ever-increasing capacity for reasoning, designing LLM-powered agents that are both functional and user-centric remains an intricate challenge. This article explores the best practices for creating AI agents that combine technical innovation with usability. We will delve into key principles and frameworks while grounding our discussion with real-world examples, demonstrating that these systems are not futuristic concepts but are tools readily transforming industries today.

Understanding AI Agents

AI agents are an 80-year-old overnight success story. The journey began in the 1950s with symbolic AI systems like the General Problem Solver, followed by expert systems in the 1980s and reactive agents in the 1990s. Today's agents are more advanced, leveraging vast data sets, huge computing power, deep learning and natural language processing to perform tasks autonomously.

Why Are Agents Needed?

Traditional robotic process automation robots are restricted by their logic flows and lack of real-time adaptability.

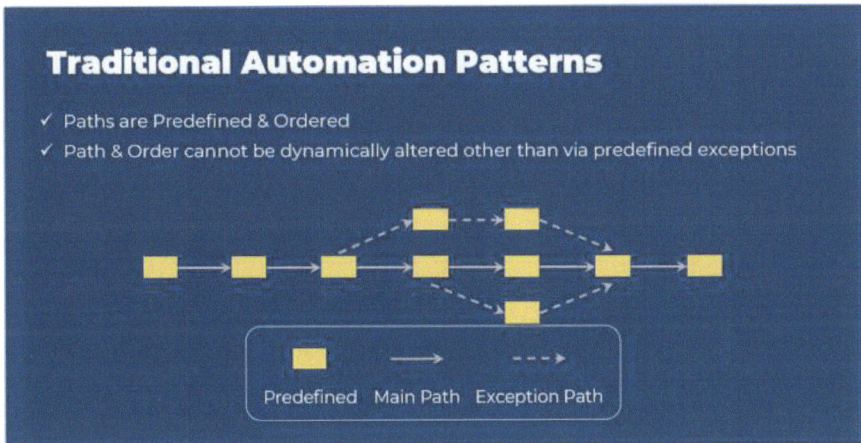

Traditional Automation Patterns

✓ Paths are Predefined & Ordered
✓ Path & Order cannot be dynamically altered other than via predefined exceptions

Predefined   Main Path   Exception Path

How many actual business scenarios look like that?

Traditional Automation Patterns (Nathaniel Palmer, Infocap).

Chatbots are limited to responding to whatever is contained within their training data. For example, even if you ask an LLM-enabled chatbot with a knowledge cut-off date about a recent event or information outside its dataset, it will either respond with a failsafe, "I'm sorry, this is outside my scope," or worse, hallucinate and provide an inaccurate answer.

Generative AI can create extraordinary new content such as video, audio, images, or text, but it cannot take action.

Such limitations starkly highlighted the need for a more dynamic business solution. Agentic AI moves beyond providing information or following rigid pre-defined paths to taking reasoning, communicating and more importantly, taking action to deliver significant business value.

For example, agents can reason about which database to query or which external tools to connect to in order to deliver a business outcome. This affords them the ability to autonomously execute tasks and act, thus showing a degree of human-like agency without the need for human guidance.

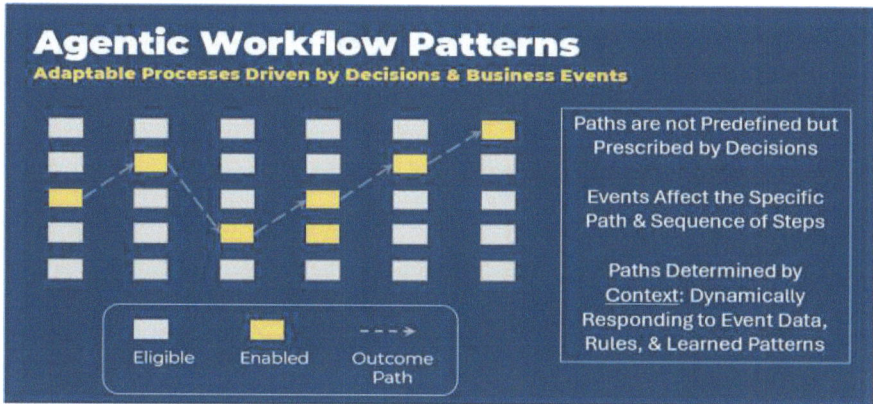

Agentic Workflow Patterns
Adaptable Processes Driven by Decisions & Business Events

Paths are not Predefined but Prescribed by Decisions

Events Affect the Specific Path & Sequence of Steps

Paths Determined by Context: Dynamically Responding to Event Data, Rules, & Learned Patterns

Eligible   Enabled   Outcome Path

Leveraging Process Analysis with Human-Centered Design

Agentic Workflow Patterns (Nathaniel Palmer, Infocap).

AI Agents are not just tools. They are autonomous enablers that transform how businesses operate, scale, and innovate. They empower enterprises to reimagine workflows, solve challenges, and create entirely new business possibilities.

Agent-Environment Interaction

A fundamental concept in agent design is the agent-environment interaction, where the agent observes the environment, takes actions, and receives feedback from a human in the loop (HITL). A simple illustration of an agent-environment interaction is a digital thermostat. A thermostat is a basic agent that observes the temperature in a room (environment), acts by adjusting the heating or cooling system, and receives feedback in the form of temperature readings. This interaction enables the thermostat to maintain a desired temperature, demonstrating a fundamental aspect of agent design.

An example of a more complicated agent would be autonomous vehicles that use sensors to navigate traffic, interpreting signals and adjusting their path dynamically. This interaction is defined by the agent's ability to respond to real-world scenarios.

A more recent real-world illustration is AutoGPT, a framework enabling agents to autonomously tackle multi-step tasks, such as managing and booking complex travel arrangements. In the case of AutoGPT, the environment is not the physical world but the digital context through access to the personal data of the user, such as schedule, budget, dietary preferences, payment options, etc. An AutoGPT-based agent can book flights, reserve hotels, and even plan itineraries based on an understanding of your personal preferences, demonstrating the power of integrating data processing, decision-making and action capabilities.

Evolution of Voice Assistants

Voice assistants like Alexa and Siri are AI agents that have evolved over time. Initially, they were programmed to rely on keyword input and pre-defined scripts to respond to user queries. Their responses were often limited and lacked a true understanding of the user's intent. However, with the incorporation of Large Language Models (LLMs), they can now better understand natural language, context, and user intent. This enables them to provide more relevant and personalized responses, vastly improving user experience in the process.

Although voice assistants have become more sophisticated, they still operate within predefined boundaries and often require explicit instructions or clarification from the user. Their success lies in simplicity and focus, highlighting the importance of a clear, user-centric goal in agent design.

Designing effective AI agents similarly starts with defining their purpose and scope. By understanding the agent-environment interaction and the complexities of real-world applications, developers can create agents that are more sophisticated, autonomous, and user-centric. Agents can then be given pre-defined goals and get left to autonomously execute the task they have been given.

Frameworks for Building AI Agents

Developing AI agents requires frameworks, tools, and methodologies. The right framework can empower developers to build advanced AI agents efficiently. For example, LangChain enables developers to string together tasks and APIs, creating complex workflows. For example, an e-commerce chatbot can leverage LangChain to answer customer queries, recommend products, and process orders seamlessly. LangFlow offers a low-code alternative for building agents with visual drag-and-drop interfaces. This approach democratizes access to AI tools, making it easier for non-technical users to develop agents.

Increasingly sophisticated and powerful low-code and no-code development platforms like Bubble and Zapier are democratizing and revolutionizing agent development, particularly for non-technical users. These platforms enable users to create agents without needing to write code. For example, a small business owner can use these tools to create a sales assistant that automates lead management.

What are the best practices to follow when selecting a framework?

When selecting a framework, consider the following factors:

1. **Flexibility**: Choose frameworks that support external tool integration, such as LangChain, for database connectivity.

2. **Ease of Use**: Go for platforms like LangFlow or low-code, no-code platforms that are beginner-friendly.

3. **Scalability**: Ensure the framework can manage growing demands, such as more API calls or expanded datasets.

4. **Secure:** Build solutions that are not only scalable but secure by default to avoid data security issues at a later date.

By considering these factors and choosing the right framework, developers can efficiently build AI agents that meet their needs.

Building Your First AI Agent

The first step in creating an AI agent is defining its core tasks. For example, a personal finance assistant could help users manage budgets by categorizing expenses and providing insights. Once the purpose is clear, developers configure APIs and frameworks to bring the agent to life.

Integration with large language models (LLMs) from the likes of Open AI, Perplexity or Anthropic, for example, is crucial for natural language understanding, enabling agents to clearly interpret user inputs. Consider a real-world example from Zapier, where an AI agent integrates with multiple platforms like Gmail and Slack, automating workflows such as drafting emails and updating team dashboards based on project progress.

Developers must also implement user feedback mechanisms to refine the agent's performance over time. For instance, agents should allow users to correct errors or provide additional information during interactions. This iterative improvement ensures the agent remains dependable and user-friendly.

Steps to Build an Agent

1. **Define the Task:** Begin with a single purpose. For example, develop a content summarizer for news articles.

2. **Select a Framework:** Use LangChain for task orchestration or LangFlow for a simplified setup.

3. **Integrate LLM APIs:** Connect your agent to OpenAI or Google APIs for language processing.

Mastering Agentic Workflow

The effectiveness of an AI agent depends on how well it manages complex tasks. This involves breaking down processes into logical steps and seamlessly coordinating them. For instance, HubSpot leverages AI agents to streamline lead nurturing. Their agents analyze user behavior, segment customers, and send personalized email campaigns—all without manual intervention.

Decomposing Tasks

Tasks must be broken into manageable subtasks. Consider an e-commerce agent responsible for processing returns:

1. Validate the user's request by checking the order ID.

2. Verify eligibility for a return based on policy rules.

3. Generate a return label and update inventory systems.

This modular approach ensures clarity and efficiency while allowing developers to isolate and troubleshoot any issues.

Seamless Collaboration

A key component of agentic workflow is enabling agents to collaborate effectively. For example, in logistics, multi-agent systems manage warehouse operations, with one agent tracking inventory, another coordinating shipping schedules, and yet another optimizing delivery routes. These agents communicate and share data in real-time to avoid bottlenecks and maximize throughput.

Error Recovery Mechanisms

Agents must also anticipate failures and implement recovery mechanisms. Imagine a scheduling agent encountering a conflict in a user's calendar. Instead of halting the process, the agent can notify the user, suggest alternate times, and resolve the issue. Such features build reliability and user trust.

Agentic Memory Management

Memory plays a critical role in an AI agent's ability to adapt and personalize interactions. Whether it is short-term memory for session-specific tasks or long-term memory for retaining user preferences, proper memory management defines the agent's utility.

Memory Types

- **Short-term Memory:** Used during active sessions. A chatbot answering customer queries remembers the context of the conversation to provide coherent responses.

- **Long-term Memory:** Retains historical data like user preferences. Spotify's AI agents use this to curate personalized playlists based on listening habits.

- **Episodic Memory:** Stores specific instances to improve decision-making. A customer service agent might recall a user's past complaints to offer tailored resolutions.

Storage and Retrieval Technologies

To implement these memory types, developers use systems like vector databases, key-value stores, or knowledge graphs.

Vector Databases

Vector databases are designed to store and manage high-dimensional vectors, which are used to represent complex data such as images, text, and audio. These databases enable efficient similarity searches, allowing developers to find the most similar vectors to a given query vector.

Vector databases are particularly useful for:

1. **Semantic search**: Finding relevant documents or data points based on their semantic meaning. An AI agent can use a vector database to search for similar products based on their descriptions and features.

2. **Recommendation systems**: Suggesting items based on their similarity to a user's preferences. A movie recommendation AI agent can use a vector database to suggest movies with similar genres, directors, or actors.

3. **Image and audio retrieval**: Finding similar images or audio files based on their visual or audio features. An AI-powered image classification agent can use a vector

database to find similar images based on their visual features.

Examples of vector databases include, Pinecone, Weaviate, Qdrant.

Key-Value Stores

Key-value stores are simple, lightweight databases that store data as a collection of key-value pairs. Each key is unique, and the corresponding value can be a string, integer, or other data type.

Key-value stores are ideal for:

1. **Caching**: Storing frequently accessed data to reduce latency. A chatbot AI agent can use a key-value store to cache user conversation history.

2. **Session management**: Storing user session data, such as login information. For instance, an e-commerce AI agent can use a key-value store to manage user shopping cart sessions.

3. **Real-time analytics**: Storing and retrieving real-time data, such as website analytics. For example, a website monitoring AI agent can use a key-value store to store and retrieve real-time website traffic data.

Examples of key-value stores include [Redis](#), [Riak](#), [AWS DynamoDB](#), etc.

Knowledge Graphs

Knowledge graphs are databases that store complex, interconnected data as a graph of entities and relationships. Each entity represents a concept, object, or individual, and the relationships represent the connections between entities.

Knowledge graphs are particularly useful for:

1. **Question answering**: Answering complex questions by traversing the graph of entities and relationships. A virtual assistant AI agent can use a knowledge graph to answer questions about user schedules, appointments, and reminders.

2. **Recommendation systems**: Suggesting items based on their relationships to other entities in the graph. A product recommendation AI agent can use a knowledge graph to suggest products based on how they compare to other products, brands, and categories.

3. **Data integration**: Integrating data from multiple sources by representing the relationships between entities. A data integration AI agent can use a knowledge graph to connect data from multiple sources, such as

customer relationship management (CRM) systems, enterprise resource planning (ERP) systems, and social media platforms.

Examples of knowledge graphs include Google's Knowledge Graph, Amazon's Product Graph, Neo4j.

Example Case Study: A language learning app deployed an AI tutor that uses episodic memory to recall a user's weak areas and suggest targeted practice sessions. This resulted in a 25% increase in user retention over six months.

Evaluating AI Agents

Designing an AI agent is only half the battle; evaluating its performance ensures it delivers value to users. Metrics like accuracy, response time, and decision quality are critical for assessing agent effectiveness.

Success Metrics

- **Accuracy:** How well the agent performs its tasks. For instance, a virtual shopping assistant should recommend products that match the user's preferences.

- **Response Time:** The speed at which the agent processes and replies. Studies show that users expect responses within 2 seconds for chatbots.

- **Decision Quality:** The ability to provide insightful and helpful outputs. A financial planning agent should offer actionable investment advice based on real-time data.

Evaluation Techniques

- **Context Retention:** Testing how well the agent remembers previous interactions.

- **Dataset Benchmarking:** Comparing the agent's performance across various datasets to ensure consistency.

For example, OpenAI evaluates its ChatGPT models by testing them on benchmarks like MMLU (Massive Multitask Language Understanding) to gauge their reasoning and context-handling capabilities.

Iterative Refinement

Evaluation is not a one-time activity. Agents should improve through user feedback loops. For example, a healthcare triage agent can adjust its recommendations based on patient feedback, ensuring better accuracy and patient satisfaction over time.

Multi-Agent Collaboration

AI agents rarely operate in isolation. Multi-agent systems bring together specialized agents to solve complex problems collaboratively. NASA's Mars Rover missions use a multi-agent framework where individual agents manage tasks like navigation, analysis, and communication with mission control.

Collaboration Strategies

- **Role Specialization:** Assigning unique roles to agents, such as one for data analysis and another for decision-making.

- **Dependency Management:** Ensuring agents coordinate seamlessly without conflicts or delays.

Communication Protocols

Agents use protocols like gRPC or custom APIs to exchange information. For instance, in a smart home system, the thermostat, lighting, and security agents communicate to optimize energy usage while maintaining safety.

Exploring Agentic Retrieval-Augmented Generation (RAG)

RAG (Retrieval-Augmented Generation) is a prominent architecture for building sophisticated AI agents.

When an input (prompt or audio) is received, the agent first assesses whether the request can be fulfilled solely based on its existing knowledge. For example, a request to "polish a piece of clumsy text" can often be addressed directly without external data retrieval.

However, if the input requires real-time information (e.g., "What's the current weather?") or access to specific personal data (e.g., "When is my next meeting?"), the agent initiates the retrieval (R) step. This involves searching relevant sources or querying an appropriate database:

- **Web search:** For real-time information like weather, news, or stock prices.

- **Personal data sources:** Calendars, contacts, email, and other personal information stored in cloud services.

- **External knowledge bases:** Specialized databases, academic journals, or company-specific documents.

- The retrieved data is then carefully **augmented (A)**. This involves:

- **Contextualization:** Integrating the retrieved data into the original input to provide the LLM with a comprehensive understanding of the request.

- **Enrichment:** Adding relevant background information, definitions, or common-sense knowledge to enhance the LLM's understanding.

- **Formatting:** Presenting the information in a structured format that the LLM can effectively process.

The augmented input is fed into the LLM for generation (G). The LLM leverages this enriched information to produce a more accurate, informative, and relevant response.

In the RAG pipeline, LLMs serve multiple functions beyond basic text generation. They are used for complex reasoning tasks, like determining which database to query and selecting appropriate output formats—whether that's text, images, videos, or specific documents like hotel booking confirmations. LLMs are particularly valuable for these reasoning tasks because the potential decision paths are too numerous and nuanced to be efficiently managed through traditional programming logic.

Context Handling and Memory

A core aspect of RAG involves handling large knowledge bases and delivering precise, context-aware answers. For example, Notion AI uses RAG to help users summarize lengthy documents, retrieve relevant sections, and generate actionable summaries based on user queries.

Building Robust Pipelines

RAG workflows involve retrieving data, processing it with language models, and generating responses. These pipelines can be optimized by:

- Integrating APIs for real-time data retrieval.

- Using embeddings to store and index contextual data for efficient search.

Feedback Loops and Learning

Feedback loops refine agent performance. For instance, Duolingo's AI tutor uses user responses to improve its learning path suggestions. This iterative refinement ensures the agent evolves to meet user expectations.

For example, in healthcare, Infermedica, a medical AI platform, employs RAG to provide symptom analysis and generate diagnostic suggestions. By accessing up-to-date medical databases, it improves the accuracy and relevance of its advice, saving time for both patients and physicians.

Ethics, Privacy, and Trust in Agent Design

As AI agents become more autonomous, addressing ethical concerns and fostering trust is paramount. Users need to feel confident that agents prioritize privacy and operate transparently.

Challenges in Ethics and Privacy

AI agents face risks such as bias, misuse, and breaches of user data. Consider the controversy surrounding facial recognition agents. While effective in identifying individuals, these systems have faced backlash for racial bias and lack of accountability.

Best Practices for Trustworthy Design

- **Transparency:** Clearly communicate what the agent can and cannot do. For example, Google's AI-powered Gemini explicitly states its limitations to users during interactions.

- **Privacy-First Approaches:** Minimize data collection and use encryption to safeguard sensitive information. Apple's **Siri** processes many queries locally on the device, reducing reliance on cloud servers.

- **Ethical Guidelines:** Implement frameworks like OpenAI's guidelines for responsible AI development, ensuring fairness and accountability.

Regulatory Considerations

Governments and organizations worldwide are developing AI regulations. Adhering to standards like GDPR in Europe or similar frameworks ensures compliance and user trust.

For example, financial AI agents deployed by Plaid adhere to strict security measures, encrypting user data while offering seamless banking integrations. This approach has built trust among users managing sensitive financial information.

The Future of Agentic AI

AI agents are poised to become integral to our lives. Success depends on developing ecosystems that address current limitations and unlock new possibilities.

Integrated Ecosystems: Agents, Sims, and Assistants

Future systems may combine agents, Sims (representing user preferences and behaviors), and Assistants (conducting agent interactions). This layered approach, proposed by Shah and White, ensures tasks are handled with precision, efficiency, and personalization.

Example Vision:

Imagine a smart home ecosystem where Sims learn a user's habits (like sleep schedules or preferred temperatures). Agents manage individual tasks, such as adjusting lighting or preparing morning routines, while an Assistant ensures all systems work harmoniously.

Standardization and Scalability

To make agentic AI dependable, we must focus on standardizing protocols and creating scalable systems. An "agent store," like app stores, could provide tested agents that users and developers trust.

Personalization and Trust

AI agents will get smarter and more personal, learning from past interactions and making better choices. Ethical AI that fits user needs will be key.

For example, in education, platforms like Coursera envision AI agents that not only recommend courses but also adapt content delivery based on a learner's pace and style, offering a truly personalized experience.

Conclusion

AI agents are reshaping industries, driving efficiency, and enhancing user experiences in ways previously unimaginable. However, designing effective agents requires more than just technical expertise. It calls for user-centricity, robust evaluation, and a commitment to ethics and trust.

By integrating frameworks, managing workflows, and addressing challenges like privacy and scalability, developers can create agents that deliver real value. As we move toward an ecosystem of agents, Sims, and Assistants, the potential for AI-driven transformation becomes limitless.

The future of AI agents is here. It is not science fiction; it is the technology of today paving the way for tomorrow.

References

- Agents Are Not Enough

- General agent design best practices | Dialogflow ES | Google Cloud

- What is a Vector Database & How Does it Work? Use Cases + Examples | Pinecone

- Coursera announces new AI content and innovations to help HR and learning leaders drive organizational agility amid relentless disruption - Coursera Blog

- Our approach to AI safety | OpenAI

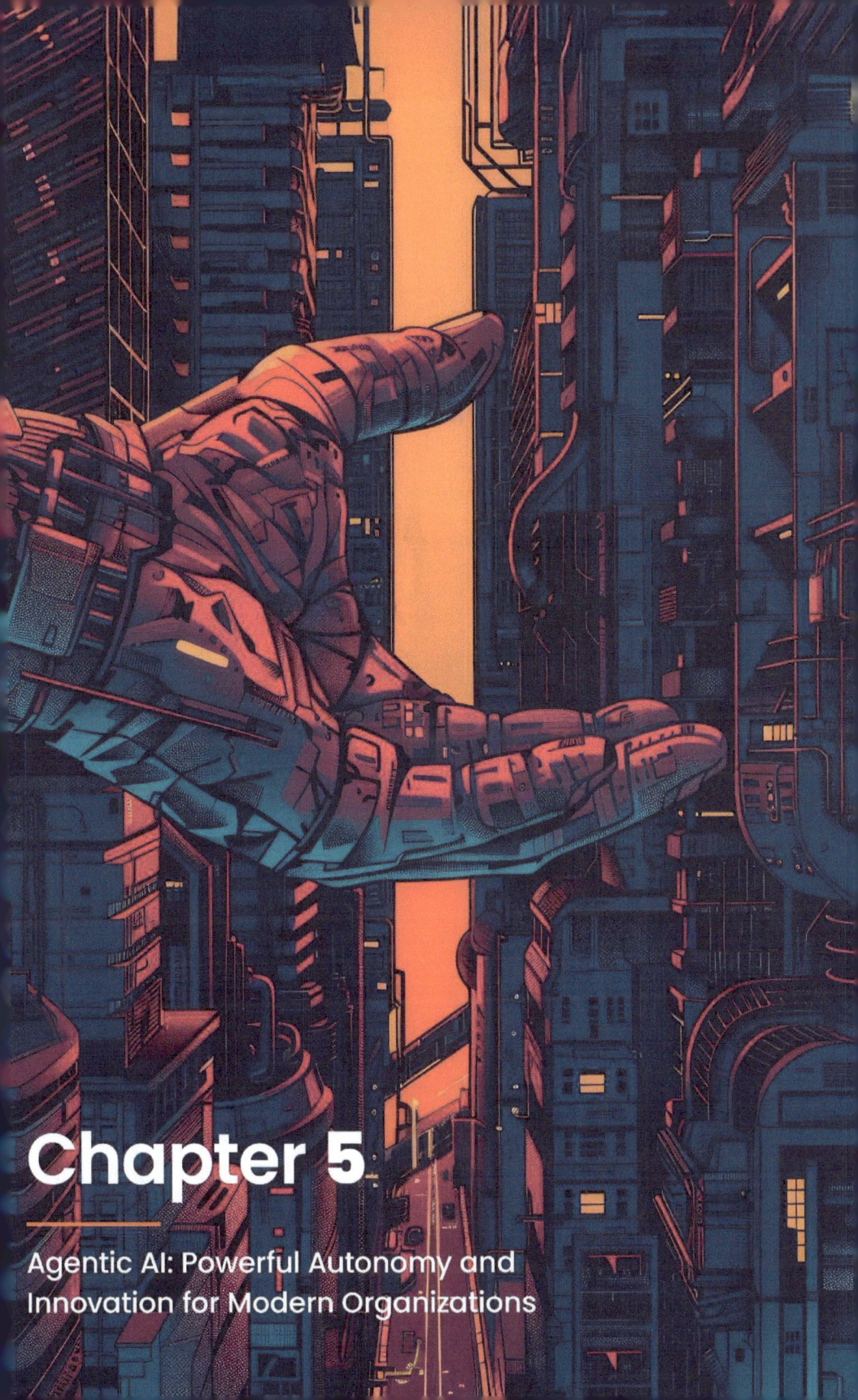

Chapter 5

Agentic AI: Powerful Autonomy and Innovation for Modern Organizations

Agentic AI: Powerful Autonomy and Innovation for Modern Organizations

In just a few decades, we have witnessed a remarkable technological evolution. From floppy disks to AI, innovation has reshaped our world. Now, Agentic AI is emerging as a potential game-changer, offering unparalleled autonomy and decision-making capabilities. Imagine your very own AI agent selflessly collaborating with you not only taking on the repetitive, time-consuming tasks that hold you back but enriching and elevating your performance to new heights.

Unlike traditional automation technologies like Robotic Process Automation (RPA), Agentic AI operates independently, taking on complex tasks without constant human oversight. This article explores the potential of Agentic AI, its distinctions from other automation forms, and its transformative impact on industries.

What is Agentic Artificial Intelligence?

Agentic Artificial Intelligence is a unique AI system that operates autonomously, making decisions and taking actions without direct human control. It is like a proactive assistant, taking on greater responsibility for achieving specific goals. These systems anticipate and respond to user needs and adapt to new information and changing circumstances in real-time.

Agentic systems make decisions, interact with their environment, and take actions independently from direct human control or intervention. These systems anticipate and respond to user needs and adapt to new information and changing circumstances in real-time.

For instance, imagine an AI-driven investment advisor that not only monitors market conditions but also autonomously adjusts your portfolio based on real-time data and future predictions. This level of autonomy empowers organizations to make more informed decisions faster while significantly reducing the need for human oversight, ultimately driving operational efficiency and innovation.

How is Agentic AI different from Robotic Process Automation?

- **Agentic AI vs. RPA:** While both are automation technologies, Agentic AI is far more adaptable and capable of handling unforeseen situations. RPA follows pre-programmed rules, whereas Agentic AI makes its own decisions based on predefined goals.

- **Agentic AI vs. Generative AI:** Agentic AI focuses on decision-making and action-taking, while Generative AI specializes in creating new content like text, images, or music.

Unlike RPA software, agentic AI is not bound by pre-programmed actions, inspiring a new wave of possibilities in the business world. It has the remarkable ability to adapt to new situations that its developers did not explicitly code. This means agentic AI can manage unforeseen events by making its own decisions as long as they align with its particular goals or objectives. This adaptability provides a sense of reassurance that agentic AI can manage unexpected situations effectively.

Think of a self-driving car navigating and making decisions on its own or a conversational AI customer service agent handling inquiries without human intervention. These examples illustrate how Agentic AI makes decisions based on predefined goals and adapts as needed to meet diverse customer needs.

How does Agentic AI differ from Generative AI?

Agentic AI and **Generative AI** are distinct branches of artificial intelligence. Agentic AI excels at decision-making and taking action, while Generative AI focuses on creating new content, such as text, images, or music, by learning from existing data.

AI agents, particularly Agentic AI, offer efficiency, scalability, and a competitive edge across various industries. From finance and healthcare to manufacturing and customer support, Agentic AI streamlines processes, reduces errors, and enables faster, informed decision-making.

In contrast, Generative AI is centered on creating new content, such as text, images, or music, by learning patterns from the existing data upon which it has been trained.

Feature	Agentic AI	Robotic Process Automation (RPA)	Generative AI
Decision-Making Capability	**High -** Can adapt to new situations	**Low -** Follows predefined rules	**Medium -** Generates content based on data
Autonomy Level	**High -** Operates with minimal human oversight	**Low -** Requires precise programming	**Medium -** Requires human input to define tasks
Learning and Adaptation	**Yes -** Continuously learns and improves	**No -** Static processes	**Yes -** Learns patterns to create new content
Primary Applications	Autonomous systems, complex decision-making	Routine task automation	Content creation (text, images, music)

Agentic AI, RPA, and Generative AI

Do Agentic Systems Operate Entirely Without Human Oversight?

Some agentic AI systems operate with a certain level of autonomy but still allow humans to intervene in critical decision-making processes (known as humans in the Loop. Others function completely independently (known as "fully autonomous AI").

Now, let us delve into the two types of agentic AI.

Humans in the Loop (HITL)

First, we have 'Humans in the Loop' (HITL), a concept that brings human expertise into the AI's decision-making process.

Medicine is complex, but an AI system can be trained on large datasets of medical records, imaging, and patient histories to autonomously analyze a new patient's data, such as X-rays, blood test results, symptoms, and then suggest potential diagnoses. Based on its analysis, the AI might indicate to a doctor that a patient is prone to a specific disease (e.g., pneumonia) and recommend a course of action (e.g., further testing and treatment options).

A doctor can then either agree or disagree with the AI's assessment after looking at other factors that the AI might not fully grasp, such as subtle nuances in patient history, ethical considerations, or personal patient interactions. In this case, the doctor makes the final decision on the diagnosis and treatment plan, balancing the AI's data-driven insights with their professional judgment and expertise. In this example, human oversight (i.e., a medical professional) ensures that decisions are carefully reviewed and validated by a medical professional.

Fully Autonomous Artificial Intelligence

In contrast, fully autonomous AI agents are designed to operate, make decisions, and take actions without human input. Take the example of an autonomous underwater vehicle (AUV) used for deep-sea exploration that operates in environments where human intervention is neither possible nor practical due to extreme conditions like high pressure, low visibility, or communication limitations. AUVs have sensors, cameras, sonar, and AI-driven navigation systems. Once deployed into the ocean, they can operate for lengthy periods without any direct human control. The vehicle follows pre-set missions but can also make decisions on its own based on real-time data.

For example, suppose an AUV is tasked with mapping the ocean floor. In that case, it will autonomously navigate underwater terrain, avoid obstacles, and collect data on its surroundings if the AUV encounters unexpected situations, such as discovering a previously unknown geological feature or an underwater current that could affect its path. Rather than stopping, the AUV autonomously adjusts its course and behavior without needing to communicate with humans for instructions.

To recap:

- **Humans in the Loop (HITL):** In healthcare, an AI system can analyze patient data and suggest diagnoses. A doctor then reviews the AI's recommendations, considering additional factors before making the final decision.

- **Fully Autonomous AI:** Autonomous underwater vehicles (AUVs) operate in extreme deep-sea environments where human intervention is not feasible. They follow pre-set missions but also make independent decisions based on real-time data.

Why are companies so interested in AI agents?

AI agents, particularly Agentic AI, have the potential to deliver efficiency, scalability, and competitive advantage across various industries. Just as companies invested in RPA, functions like finance, human resources, and customer support could leverage Agentic AI to automate tasks like payroll processing, invoice management, and employee onboarding, inspiring new possibilities in the business world.

For example, in finance, agentic AI could continuously analyze data to provide real-time budgeting, forecasting, and scenario analysis. It enables more accurate and dynamic financial planning. It could also autonomously monitor transactions, detect anomalies, and predict potential fraud with great precision, reducing financial losses.

Agentic AI could assist in diagnosis and treatment planning in healthcare, better organize shift work in factories and contact centers, optimize the production processes in manufacturing, and enhance safety and efficiency in transportation.

- [Oracle](#)'s Shift Scheduling Assistant optimizes shift schedules while managing compliance and employee preferences.

In HR, agentic AI could autonomously manage the entire recruitment process, from screening resumes and conducting initial interviews to ranking candidates based on fit and predicting their potential success in the role. This would streamline the hiring process, reduce bias, and ensure that the best candidates are selected efficiently.

- [Workday](#)'s Recruiter Agent helps manage employee development with AI-driven Succession Agents. It is transforming leadership development by identifying future leaders and creating AI-driven development plans.

In customer support, agentic AI could power advanced conversational AI chatbots that autonomously handle customer inquiries, from troubleshooting technical issues to processing returns and refunds. Conversational AI chatbots could learn from interactions to improve their accuracy and efficiency.

- Salesforce's Agentforce handles customer service inquiries, optimizes marketing campaigns, and qualifies sales leads autonomously.

The potential applications of Agentic AI are vast and diverse. If we embrace the richness of the technology if, we resist the temptation to simply 'embalm' existing processes in a new AI wrapper.

The Future of Autonomy: Unlocking the Potential of Agentic AI

Agentic AI represents a significant leap forward in the evolution of artificial intelligence, offering a level of autonomy and adaptability that sets it apart from traditional automation technologies. Its ability to operate independently, make complex decisions, and adapt to new information in real-time opens up unprecedented opportunities across various industries. From finance to healthcare, manufacturing to customer support, Agentic AI is set to revolutionize how businesses operate, driving efficiency, scalability, and innovation IF we rethink business using Generative AI.

As with any emerging technology, the rise of Agentic AI brings with it a set of challenges and ethical concerns. Issues such as data privacy, the potential for AI bias, and the need for clear accountability in AI-driven decisions must be addressed to ensure the responsible deployment of these systems. Companies investing in Agentic AI should prioritize transparency and ethical standards to build trust and mitigate risks.

As organizations continue to explore and integrate Agentic AI, the technology promises to enhance operational processes and redefine the relationship between humans and machines. By taking on more complex tasks with minimal oversight, Agentic AI allows human workers to focus on higher-level strategic initiatives, ultimately leading to more informed decision-making and improved outcomes.

In a rapidly evolving technological landscape, adopting Agentic AI could be a key factor in maintaining a competitive edge. Companies embracing this technology are likely to lead innovation, navigating the complexities of the modern world with greater agility and precision. The future of Agentic AI is bright, and its impact on industries will undoubtedly be transformative if we successfully adopt it.

References:

- What Is Agentic AI & Is It the Next Big Thing?

- Agentic Process Automation (APA): Revolutionizing Digital Automation with AI Agents (botnirvana.org)

- A new AI Era: Agentic AI. In the landscape of artificial... | by Humans.ai

- Agentic AI: The Next Evolution of Enterprise AI | Moveworks

- How Does Agentic AI Differ from Traditional AI? | by carlos lacerda | Medium

- The promise and peril of 'agentic AI' - Computerworld

- What is Agentic AI? | LinkedIn

Chapter 6

Leading in the Era
of Human-AI Collaboration

6

Leading in the Era of Human-AI Collaboration

As artificial intelligence (AI) continues to redefine industries, leadership in the AI age demands an entirely new set of skills and strategies. The integration of AI agents, systems capable of autonomous decision-making, into human teams is no longer a futuristic concept but a pressing reality. From healthcare diagnostics to algorithmic trading and autonomous product development, these agents are reshaping how teams operate. For leaders, this presents a unique challenge: navigating the interplay between human creativity and AI efficiency while fostering trust and collaboration. Leaders must balance AI's operational benefits with its human impact in organizations. These gains come only after proactively addressing team concerns about job displacement and implementing robust training programs to ensure seamless collaboration. This highlights the dual mandate for leaders: leveraging AI's capabilities while addressing its social and ethical implications.

The stakes of this leadership challenge are particularly high, given the unprecedented pace of AI advancement. Organizations that successfully integrate AI while maintaining employee engagement and well-being will emerge as industry leaders, while those that fail to address the human dimensions of AI adoption risk cultural deterioration and talent exodus.

This new paradigm requires leaders to be both technologically literate and emotionally intelligent, capable of articulating a compelling vision for human-AI collaboration while acknowledging and addressing legitimate concerns about the future of work. Moreover, leaders must cultivate an organizational culture that values continuous learning and adaptation, recognizing that the journey of AI integration is not a one-time transformation but an ongoing evolution.

How AI Agents Reshape Team Dynamics

Redefining Roles and Responsibilities

AI agents bring new dynamics to the workplace, fundamentally altering traditional roles. For example, in financial services, trading desks are increasingly staffed by a combination of human traders and algorithmic agents. While humans focus on strategy and risk assessment, AI agents execute trades at lightning speed, adapting to market fluctuations in real-time.

This division of labor allows humans to focus on creative, high-value tasks while delegating repetitive or data-intensive functions to AI. However, the shift requires leaders to clearly define roles, set expectations, and ensure that both human and AI contributions are valued. Failure to do so can lead to confusion, inefficiency, and resistance to change.

Enhancing Productivity and Innovation

AI agents excel at processing vast amounts of data and identifying patterns that humans might overlook. In manufacturing, for instance, predictive maintenance systems powered by AI agents can forecast equipment failures, reducing downtime by up to 50% while increasing machine lifespan by 20%. This enables teams to focus on innovation rather than firefighting operational issues.

Moreover, the presence of AI agents can inspire human team members to think differently. By overseeing routine tasks, AI frees up time for humans to explore creative solutions, driving innovation. Leaders must create an environment where this symbiotic relationship thrives, encouraging experimentation and cross-functional collaboration.

Sectoral Impact of Combined Teams

Retail: Optimizing Inventory Management

Take the case of Daka, a company that implemented an AI Replenisher to optimize inventory management. This AI-driven solution reduced overstock by 47% through SKU-level sales forecasting and customized replenishment strategies. Leaders in retail faced challenges such as addressing team concerns about job displacement and implementing robust training programs. By doing so, they ensured seamless collaboration between human teams and AI systems, demonstrating the tangible benefits of adopting AI-driven solutions.

Beyond inventory, AI agents are enabling personalized customer experiences. By analyzing purchasing patterns and customer preferences, these systems help retailers offer tailored product recommendations, boosting sales significantly. Leaders who embrace this dual capability, operational optimization, and customer engagement can position their organizations at the forefront of retail innovation.

Healthcare: AI-Driven Diagnostics and Patient Care Teams

In healthcare, AI agents are transforming diagnostics and patient care. For example, Google Health's AI has demonstrated the ability to detect breast cancer in mammograms with higher accuracy than human radiologists.

94

At Moorfields Eye Hospital in London, AI-powered tools have been used to diagnose eye diseases as effectively as leading specialists, significantly speeding up treatment decisions. By integrating these agents into care teams, hospitals improve diagnostic speed and accuracy, enabling earlier interventions.

However, the success of such systems hinges on leadership. Effective leaders ensure that AI agents complement, rather than replace, human expertise. They invest in training programs to help clinicians interpret AI-generated insights and foster a culture of collaboration where human judgment and AI precision work in tandem.

Leaders in healthcare are also exploring AI's potential for administrative efficiency. By automating tasks such as patient scheduling and billing, AI agents free up medical staff to focus on patient care. This dual focus on clinical and operational benefits is reshaping how hospitals deliver value to patients.

Finance: Risk Management and Algorithmic Trading

The financial sector has been at the forefront of adopting AI agents. Algorithmic trading systems now manage most global financial transactions, executing trades in milliseconds based on real-time data analysis. For instance, JPMorgan Chase's AI-driven COiN (Contract Intelligence) platform processes legal documents and contracts at speeds unachievable by humans, saving the company 360,000 hours of work annually. Similarly,

AI agents in risk management can model complex scenarios to predict potential market disruptions.

For leaders in finance, the challenge lies in balancing speed and control. While AI agents excel at rapid decision-making, they can also magnify systemic risks if not effectively managed. Leaders must implement robust oversight mechanisms, ensuring that AI actions align with organizational objectives and regulatory requirements.

Additionally, the rise of generative AI in financial advisory services is transforming how institutions engage with clients. Personalized investment strategies powered by AI are democratizing access to sophisticated financial planning tools, a shift that requires leaders to adapt their value propositions and service models.

Technology: Autonomous Systems in Product Development

In technology-driven industries, AI agents are integral to innovation. For instance, Tesla uses AI not only for its autonomous driving features but also for optimizing battery performance and enhancing manufacturing processes. AI-powered design tools like Autodesk's generative design software have enabled organizations to create innovative prototypes and products with unprecedented efficiency, significantly reducing design times.

Leadership in this context involves fostering a culture of experimentation. By encouraging teams to embrace AI as a collaborative partner, leaders can drive innovation while mitigating the risks associated with over-reliance on technology. Transparency and open communication are critical to building trust in AI-driven processes.

Leadership Skills in the AI Age

Balancing Technical Know-How with Emotional Intelligence

Leadership in the AI age demands a blend of technical and emotional skills. While understanding the capabilities and limitations of AI agents is essential, emotional intelligence (EQ) is equally critical. Leaders must navigate the fears and anxieties that often accompany AI adoption, addressing concerns about job security and fairness.

Consider a multinational corporation that introduced AI agents to streamline customer service. Initial resistance was high, with employees fearing redundancy. The CEO's transparent communication, combined with initiatives to reskill affected employees, helped build trust and acceptance, leading to a 40% improvement in customer satisfaction scores.

Leading Through Uncertainty and Rapid Innovation

The pace of AI development means that leaders must be comfortable with ambiguity. Traditional decision-making processes, which rely on exhaustive data and analysis, may not suffice in this fast-moving landscape. Instead, leaders must adopt agile methodologies, iterating quickly and learning from failures.

One effective strategy is to pilot AI initiatives on a small scale before scaling them organization-wide. This approach minimizes risk while providing valuable insights into how AI agents can be integrated into teams. Leaders who embrace a growth mindset and encourage experimentation are better positioned to succeed in the AI age.

Case Studies

Healthcare: Improving Patient Outcomes

At a leading hospital in Europe, AI agents were integrated into oncology care teams to analyze patient data and recommend treatment plans. The initiative reduced diagnostic errors by 25% and improved patient outcomes by 15%. However, success was not immediate. Leaders invested heavily in training programs to ensure clinicians could effectively collaborate with AI agents, emphasizing that these tools were designed to augment, not replace, human expertise.

Finance: Mitigating Risks with AI

A global investment bank implemented AI agents to enhance its risk management processes. Agents identified potential market risks hours before human analysts could, enabling the bank to mitigate losses during volatile market conditions. The leadership team's proactive approach—including regular audits of AI systems and cross-departmental collaboration—ensured that the initiative aligned with the bank's broader goals.

Technology: Accelerating Innovation

A tech startup used AI agents to optimize its product development cycle, reducing time-to-market by 30%. Leaders fostered a collaborative environment where human designers and AI tools worked together, generating innovative solutions that would have been impossible with traditional methods alone. By emphasizing transparency and continuous learning, the leadership team built trust in the AI-driven process, securing buy-in from all stakeholders.

The Ethical and Social Dimensions

Ensuring Fairness, Equity, and Accountability

The adoption of AI agents raises ethical questions about fairness, equity, and accountability. Bias in AI algorithms can perpetuate systemic inequalities, while opaque decision-making processes undermine trust. Leaders have a critical role to play in addressing these challenges.

One best practice is to establish ethical oversight committees that include diverse stakeholders. These committees can review AI systems for potential biases, ensure compliance with ethical standards, and promote transparency. Leaders must also advocate for policies that hold AI developers accountable, fostering public trust in human-AI collaboration.

Building Public Trust in Human-AI Collaboration

Public perception of AI significantly impacts its adoption. High-profile failures, such as biased hiring algorithms or autonomous vehicle accidents, have eroded trust in AI systems. Leaders must proactively address these concerns by communicating the benefits and limitations of AI agents clearly and honestly.

Community engagement is another effective strategy. By involving end-users in the design and implementation of AI systems, organizations can build systems that better meet societal needs, enhancing trust and acceptance.

Future Directions

The Role of Leaders in Guiding Societal Acceptance of AI

As AI agents become more pervasive, leaders will play a pivotal role in shaping societal attitudes toward these technologies. This involves not only advocating for ethical AI but also preparing the workforce for an AI-driven future. Reskilling programs, educational initiatives, and public awareness campaigns will be critical in ensuring that AI benefits are broadly shared.

Vision for Leadership in 2030 and Beyond

Looking ahead, leadership in the AI age will evolve significantly. By 2030, leaders will oversee teams where AI agents are as integral as human employees. The ability to foster collaboration, drive innovation, and navigate ethical complexities will define successful leadership.

One emerging trend is the rise of "digital mentors," AI agents designed to support leaders by providing real-time insights and recommendations. These tools will enable leaders to make more informed decisions, but they will also require leaders to critically evaluate AI-driven suggestions, ensuring alignment with organizational values.

Conclusion

Leadership in the age of AI agents is a delicate balancing act. It requires technical expertise, emotional intelligence, and a forward-looking vision to harness the potential of AI while addressing its challenges. By fostering collaboration between humans and AI agents, leaders can unlock unprecedented levels of productivity and innovation, paving the way for a future where technology and humanity thrive together.

Chapter 7

Implementing and Scaling Agentic AI:
A Comprehensive Framework
for Organizational Success

Implementing and Scaling Agentic AI: A Comprehensive Framework for Organizational Success

The emergence of Agentic AI brings along with it the potential to radically change how organizations operate, innovate, and create value. AI systems to date have been great at handling pre-defined, specific tasks. However, Agentic AI is equipped to make decisions, act upon complex objectives, and continually learn and improve. For organizations, this presents opportunities to enhance efficiency, drive innovation, and gain competitive advantages. Important to note, however, that this may also introduce new challenges that demand deeper deliberation and new strategies.

Many organizations are excited about Agentic AI's transformative potential, but few have done the groundwork of implementing frameworks for AI deployment and governance.

The Cisco AI Readiness Index highlights that while 97% of organizations feel increased urgency to adopt AI, only 14% are fully prepared (labeled as "Pacesetters"). Why is there a gap between aspiration and execution? Perhaps this calls attention to uncertainties in governance, organizational readiness, and scaling complexities.

Organizations face many challenges in their Agentic AI journey. First, they must establish robust governance frameworks that ensure responsible AI deployment while maintaining operational efficiency. Second, they need to transform their existing processes and workforce to integrate AI agents into operations. Finally, they must develop strategies for scaling these initiatives across their enterprise while maintaining performance, security, and ethical standards to deliver AI at scale.

Governance: Building a Foundation of Trust

An effective governance framework has three primary layers: strategic oversight, operational management, and technical implementation. The strategic layer, typically involving board members and executives, sets the overall direction and risk appetite for AI initiatives. The operational layer translates these strategic objectives into practical policies and procedures, while the technical layer ensures proper implementation and monitoring of AI systems.

Integration with existing corporate governance requires scrutiny of current processes and policies. Organizations must assess how AI governance aligns with other governance frameworks like IT governance, data governance, and risk management. This alignment ensures consistency in decision-making and prevents potential conflicts or redundancies.

Sound leadership and board oversight are crucial for successful AI governance. Boards must be mindful of the opportunities and risks associated with Agentic AI, making informed decisions about resource allocation, risk tolerance, and strategic direction. This often requires upskilling of board members and establishing dedicated AI oversight committees.

Accountability Systems

Accountability is not a mere buzzword when it comes to Agentic AI systems. You need systems that spell out *who* is responsible for every aspect of your AI's life cycle, from high-level strategy to the nitty-gritty of day-to-day operations. Without this, you are driving a self-driving car without a map.

What Does Accountability Look Like?

Imagine a logistics company implementing AI to optimize delivery routes. The AI system might inadvertently create unfair delivery patterns. For example, if the algorithm optimizes purely for profit, it could end up providing faster service to wealthy neighborhoods while reducing deliveries to lower-income areas. This raises important questions about who bears responsibility: Is it the developers who created the algorithm? The company executives who approved its use? Or the operations managers who implement the system? This scenario illustrates why clear accountability frameworks need to be established before deploying AI systems that impact public services.

Accountability ensures there is a structure to manage such dilemmas. Here is how it works:

1. **Executive Sponsors**: Think of them as the visionaries. They make sure the AI strategy aligns with the long-term business goals. For example, when UPS rolled out its ORION route optimization system, top executives made sure it supported their sustainability objectives.

2. **Program Managers**: Program managers oversee the implementation of AI systems that align with business goals. Their responsibilities include monitoring AI deployment, coordinating between teams, and addressing any operational challenges. For instance, if an AI model designed for customer demand prediction in a retail chain begins generating inaccurate forecasts, such as underestimating demand for a popular product or overstocking slow-moving items, the program manager

steps in to recalibrate the system. They work with data scientists to fine-tune algorithms, adjust training data, and refine predictive models to prevent disruptions in the supply chain.

3. **Technical Leads**: The coders and engineers. They are the ones tweaking algorithms and ensuring the AI behaves as intended. At Tesla, technical leads continuously update the Autopilot system based on real-world data, ensuring continued robustness of the self-driving Tesla's.

4. **Ethics Committees**: The conscience of the operation. Let us say an AI hiring tool starts faring certain demographics. Ethics committees help identify and address such biases before they become PR disasters. Organizations must ask themselves how they will prevent AI-driven bias or discrimination and what safeguards they will put in place to mitigate these risks.

Managing Business Risks Without Losing Sleep

Risk management in AI is not just about avoiding catastrophes. It is about staying agile in a rapidly evolving landscape. Regular risk assessments can flag early signs of issues, like an algorithm drifting away from expected behavior. For instance, a hiring AI might gradually introduce demographic biases, or a recommendation system could start suggesting increasingly extreme content. These assessments allow organizations to identify and correct minor deviations before they escalate into significant problems, ensuring AI systems remain dependable, ethical, and aligned with their original objectives.

For instance, financial institutions deploying fraud detection AI run constant tests to ensure the system doesn't start flagging legitimate transactions by accident. And when risks do emerge, escalation should ensure that the right people are looped in fast to ensure there is no fumbling around in a crisis.

Handling Incidents: The Blueprint

Incidents will happen, whether it is a technical glitch or an ethical oops. The key to handling incidents is having airtight protocols in place.

For example, when OpenAI detected ChatGPT's privacy bug in 2023, they had a response team ready to contain the issue, communicate with stakeholders, and roll out a patch within days. Their transparency earned them trust instead of backlash.

A comprehensive incident response protocol should include:

- **Clear Definitions**: What counts as a "critical failure"?

- **Response Teams**: Who jumps in when things go south?

- **Post-Incident Learning**: How do we make sure it does not happen again?

With real-world stakes and clear accountability, organizations can turn AI into a powerful ally instead of a rogue element.

Transparency and Explainability

Transparent AI systems are essential for building trust and ensuring accountability. Organizations must establish comprehensive documentation practices that track key aspects of AI development, including system deployment decisions, training data sources, pre-processing methods, model architecture, and parameter choices. Additionally, performance metrics, validation results, and any changes or updates to AI systems should be meticulously recorded.

To further enhance accountability, audit trails and logging systems must capture all significant AI system decisions, user interactions, performance metrics, compliance with ethical guidelines, and resource usage data.

Effective stakeholder communication is also crucial, as diverse groups have distinct information needs, technical teams require in-depth system details, business users need operational insights, customers seek assurance regarding AI's role, and regulators demand compliance evidence.

By implementing these measures, organizations can foster transparency, maintain ethical AI practices, and build confidence among users and stakeholders.

Ethics and Compliance

Creating ethical AI guidelines should be a collaborative process that involves input from various stakeholders, including policymakers, industry experts, and affected communities. Key considerations include ensuring fairness and non-discrimination, maintaining transparency and accountability, upholding privacy protection standards, assessing environmental impact, and fostering social responsibility. By incorporating these principles, organizations can develop AI systems that operate responsibly and align with societal values.

Bias detection and mitigation require continuous attention to prevent unintended consequences. Organizations must conduct regular audits of AI system decisions to identify potential biases, ensure the use of diverse training data, and implement bias testing protocols. Additionally, effective correction mechanisms should be in place to address identified issues, along with ongoing monitoring of long-term impacts to ensure AI systems remain fair and unbiased over time.

AI governance must align with established industry-specific regulations, data protection laws, and AI-specific legislation, as well as adhere to international standards and reporting requirements. Compliance with these frameworks not only ensures legal adherence but also enhances trust among users and stakeholders.

To meet or exceed industry benchmarks, organizations should adopt relevant ISO standards, comply with industry-specific frameworks, and actively participate in AI governance initiatives. Regular assessments against best practices, coupled with continuous improvement processes, ensure that AI systems remain ethical, transparent, and accountable as they evolve.

Agent Transformation Projects

Strategic Planning: Setting the Stage for Success

The first step in transforming a business with Agentic AI is a comprehensive plan that aligns AI ambitions with business goals. This is like laying the foundation for a skyscraper. You cannot build upward without stability underneath.

For example, when Walmart began implementing AI for supply chain optimization, they were careful not to compromise operational integrity. They conducted an extensive readiness assessment, pinpointing inefficiencies in its inventory systems and ensuring its technology infrastructure could manage the change. This resulted in faster restocks and fewer stockouts in stores, directly improving the customer experience.

A successful approach to AI integration involves breaking ambitious goals into strategic, manageable milestones. Consider Walmart's roadmap: short-term inventory improvements, medium-term cost reductions, and a visionary long-term goal of end-to-end supply chain automation.

Process Reimagination: Rethinking Workflows

AI is not just a plug-and-play tool—it is a chance to reimagine how the work gets done. Leaders must start by analyzing every corner of their operational workflows. Where are the bottlenecks? Where could automation have the most significant impact?

For example, in response to the growing demands of modern e-commerce, DHL began reimagining its warehouse operations around 2019 to address the challenges of increased order volumes and tighter delivery deadlines. Recognizing the need for faster, more efficient fulfillment processes, DHL integrated robotics and Agentic AI into its warehouses, increasing order fulfillment rates by up to 180%. They did not simply add a robot onto an old process—they rebuilt their workflows around what the AI could do best.

Equipping People for Change

AI cannot thrive in a vacuum. People need to evolve alongside tech innovation. Organizations must identify gaps between current employee skills and the expertise needed for AI-driven roles.

John Deere developed autonomous and AI-driven machinery for precision agriculture tasks like planting and fertilizing. As these intelligent machines were put on the field, agricultural experts transitioned into roles managing AI-enhanced tractors. Employees were upskilled with training such as monitoring and maintaining intelligent machinery. The result? Higher job satisfaction and increased productivity.

As AI systems become more integrated into daily operations, new roles are emerging to ensure their effective and responsible use. AI Operations Specialists oversee the day-to-day management of AI systems, making sure they function smoothly and efficiently. Meanwhile, Human-AI Collaboration Coordinators focus on optimizing interactions between human workers and AI, facilitating seamless task handoffs and enhancing productivity. Additionally, AI Ethics Officers play a crucial role in identifying and addressing issues related to bias, fairness, and responsible AI deployment. Together, these roles reflect the growing need for specialized expertise in managing, refining, and ethically governing AI technologies in various industries.

Change Management: Leading the Charge

Rolling out AI is as much about people's hearts and minds as it is about machines. Stakeholders at every level need to buy into the vision. This human-centric approach is critical because AI transformation touches every aspect of an organization. Frontline workers may fear job displacement, middle managers might worry about changing or losing their roles, and executives may be concerned about ROI and competitive positioning. Success requires transparent communication, demonstrated value, and a clear path forward that acknowledges and addresses each concern.

For example, when the UK's NHS deployed AI for early cancer detection, it faced skepticism from staff, primarily from clinicians (e.g., radiologists and oncologists) concerned about diagnostic accuracy, as well as administrative staff anxious about potential job displacement. Leaders tackled this by highlighting success stories, like how the AI helped doctors diagnose patients faster. Forums were set up to hear concerns, ensuring staff felt heard and involved in the transformation.

The successful adoption of AI in the NHS was driven by several key factors. These included providing regular updates on progress, which helped keep staff informed and engaged, addressing uncertainties, and reinforcing trust in the technology. In addition, teams focused on celebrating quick wins, such as faster and more accurate diagnoses. Wins demonstrated the tangible benefits of AI and further encouraged its adoption. Most importantly, transparency about AI's role ensured that healthcare professionals understood it as a tool to enhance, rather than replace, their expertise. By emphasizing these strategies, NHS leaders were able to foster a collaborative environment that supported the integration of AI into clinical practice.

Technical Infrastructure: Building the Backbone

Your AI is only as good as the infrastructure that supports it. Scalable cloud systems, robust data pipelines, and airtight security are non-negotiable. For example, at the heart of Netflix's seamless viewing experience lies a sophisticated AI recommendation engine, quietly working behind the scenes to analyze billions of data points every day. This intricate system thrives on a robust and scalable infrastructure, ensuring it can manage the immense demands of its global audience. Without this carefully designed architecture, the engine would struggle to keep pace, leaving millions of users searching for their next favorite show in frustration or, more likely, moving to a competitor at the click of their mouse.

[Moveworks](#), a company specializing in AI solutions, successfully implemented Agentic AI to revolutionize IT support. AI agents were programmed to resolve IT issues, such as password resets and software installations, without the need for human intervention. This transformation led to increased efficiency, by allowing IT personnel to focus on more complex tasks, but also their increased motivation. Movework's approach exemplifies the effective integration of Agentic AI into organizational workflows, resulting in enhanced productivity and employee satisfaction.

Scaling Agentic AI: Critical Success Factors

Scaling Agentic AI successfully across an organization is not just about expanding its technical footprint. It requires strategic alignment, robust infrastructure, and a culture ready to embrace innovation. Organizations that scale AI effectively unlock new efficiencies, gain competitive advantages, and often redefine their industries. Some of these factors are listed below.

1. Strategic Alignment with Business Goals.

Scaling Agentic AI begins with aligning its capabilities with the organization's objectives. AI should be implemented where it can directly impact key performance indicators (KPIs) such as revenue growth, operational efficiency, or customer satisfaction.

For example, UPS's "ORION" system is an Agentic AI that optimizes delivery routes. By scaling this system across its fleet, UPS saved an estimated 10 million gallons of fuel annually and significantly reduced delivery times, directly supporting its goals of operational efficiency and environmental sustainability. This initiative demonstrates how tying AI systems to measurable business outcomes drives success.

2. Robust Infrastructure and Scalability

A scalable infrastructure is the backbone of Agentic AI systems. Organizations must invest in high-performance cloud computing, scalable data pipelines, and secure AI platforms to manage increasing workloads. For instance, Amazon's Agentic AI systems power its fulfillment centers by coordinating robotic arms, managing inventory, and predicting order demand. With its scalable cloud infrastructure (AWS), Amazon ensures its AI can operate seamlessly across global warehouses, handling billions of orders annually. This setup highlights the importance of infrastructure in scaling AI without disruptions.

3. Continuous Monitoring and Feedback Loops

Scaling AI is not a "set it and forget it" task. Continuous monitoring and improvement are essential to address performance gaps, emerging risks, and evolving business needs. For example, Tesla's Autopilot AI uses over-the-air updates and real-time data from millions of vehicles to continuously refine its capabilities. By actively monitoring system performance and incorporating feedback, Tesla ensures its AI remains state-of-the-art and adapts to new driving conditions.

4. Leadership and Cultural Readiness

Scaling Agentic AI requires leadership to champion its adoption and foster a culture of trust and collaboration. Leaders must clearly communicate the AI's purpose, address employee concerns, and promote its benefits.

[Ping An integrated Agentic AI](#) across its operations, using intelligent agents for tasks like fraud detection and customer service. Leadership played a critical role by transparently communicating AI's goals and ensuring employees understood how the technology would complement their roles rather than replace them. This cultural readiness facilitated a smooth scaling process, boosting both productivity and employee morale.

5. Metrics and Outcomes

Successful scaling is measurable. Organizations must track metrics like ROI, operational efficiency, error reduction, and employee adoption rates to evaluate their progress. However, failing to effectively manage metrics and outcomes can lead to costly missteps.

For instance, General Electric (GE) invested <u>over $7 billion in its Predix platform</u>, an ambitious Agentic AI system designed to predict equipment failures and optimize manufacturing processes.

Despite the promise of real-time performance data and significant savings in downtime and maintenance costs, the platform struggled due to overly ambitious goals, internal cultural resistance, and the complexity of building a comprehensive industrial ecosystem.

These challenges caused the platform to fall short of expectations, serving as a cautionary tale of how insufficient alignment with measurable outcomes can derail even the most well-funded initiatives.

Conclusion: Navigating the Future of Agentic AI

AI is already transforming how we work. To scale effectively with Agentic AI, organizations need three things: careful planning, clear goals, and strong ethics. Success comes from building robust and secure systems, encouraging new ideas, and staying focused on tangible results.

As Agentic AI continues to evolve, its impact will deepen across industries. By focusing on governance, transformation, and scaling, organizations can confidently embrace this technology, unlocking possibilities of the AI-driven future. The time to act is now, decisively, responsibly, and with a vision for what is possible.

References

- https://www.cisco.com/c/m/en_us/solutions/ai/readiness-index.html

- https://medium.com/the-tesla-digest/teslas-continuous-efficiency-revolution-the-power-of-free-software-updates-2559e7748155

- https://www.aboutamazon.com/news/operations/amazon-fulfillment-center-robotics-ai

- https://www.ibm.com/think/topics/fraud-detection

- https://www.insurancebusinessmag.com/asia/news/breaking-news/ping-an-pledges-big-data-and-ai-capabilities-to-fight-fraud-161678.aspx

- https://platformengineering.org/blog/how-general-electric-burned-7-billion-on-their-platform

Chapter 8

The Dawn of AI Agents:
New Business Opportunities and Models

8

The Dawn of AI Agents: New Business Opportunities and Models

Imagine a world where your morning coffee is brewed by an AI that knows exactly how you like it, your commute is optimized by a network of autonomous agents coordinating traffic in real-time, and your workday is streamlined by a digital assistant that not only schedules meetings but also drafts emails, analyses data, and even negotiates contracts on your behalf. While all this may sound as if it were science fiction, it is being built today.

AI agents, software programs that can understand, reason, act, and learn—are no longer confined to research labs or niche applications. They are here, and they are getting smarter. But what is even more exciting is the emergence of *compound Agentic AI systems*, where multiple AI agents collaborate to solve problems far more complex than any single agent could manage alone. Think of it as a symphony of intelligences, each playing its part to create something greater than the sum of its parts.

Agentic AI systems are bringing seismic shifts to the business world. In this chapter, we will explore the new opportunities they are creating, the innovative business models they are enabling and the challenges they are posing. Along the way, we will ground the discussion in real-world examples so you can see how this is not just theoretical in nature. It is already happening.

The Rise of AI Agents

From Narrow AI to Collaborative Intelligence

For years, AI has been defined by its narrowness. A single AI system could play chess, recommend movies, or detect fraud, but it could not do much else. Narrow AI systems were like specialized tools in a toolbox: useful but limited. Enter AI agents–programs that can not only perform specific tasks but also adapt to new situations, learn from experience, and even communicate with other agents.

For example, AutoGPT, unlike its predecessor ChatGPT, responds to individual prompts. It can autonomously break down complex tasks into smaller steps, gather information from the web, and execute actions–all without human intervention. It is like having a personal assistant who does not just follow orders but anticipates your needs and figures out how to meet them.

While AutoGPT can sometimes be unreliable and prone to getting stuck in loops or making errors, it demonstrates a critical principle: AI agents can, in principle, operate autonomously, iterating on tasks and learning from their mistakes. This opens the door to a future where AI agents can manage increasingly complex and open-ended challenges, even if today's implementations are still a work in progress.

Consider Google's DeepMind and its work on multi-agent systems, such as AlphaFold for protein folding or AlphaStar for StarCraft II. These systems combine multiple AI models and techniques to tackle complex tasks that require collaboration and adaptation. For instance, AlphaStar uses a combination of reinforcement learning, imitation learning, and multi-agent training can master a game as intricate as StarCraft II.

While not a multi-agent system in the same sense, AlphaFold highlights how combining multiple AI techniques (e.g., neural networks, evolutionary algorithms) can achieve breakthroughs in complex domains such as protein folding.

By pooling their strengths, these agents can solve problems that would stump any single model alone. It is a bit like the

Avengers: individually powerful but unstoppable when they team up.

Real-World Use Cases: AI Agents in Action

Let us look at some examples to illustrate the many sectors in which Agentic AI now operates.

1. **Healthcare: AI Doctors on Call.** In 2023, the startup Hippocratic AI emerged, focusing on developing AI agents designed to assist healthcare professionals. The company aims to create AI systems that manage routine tasks such as patient intake, symptom analysis, and post-discharge follow-ups. Importantly, Hippocratic AI emphasizes that its technology is intended to augment, not replace, humans but to free them to focus on more complex cases.

2. **Retail: The Personal Shopper of the Future.** Amazon's Alexa has evolved from a voice assistant to a full-fledged AI agent. Imagine telling Alexa, "Plan a dinner party for six," and having it not only suggest recipes but also order ingredients, adjust the quantities based on dietary restrictions, and even send invitations to your guests. This may sound like a distant dream but the direction of Alexa's development, as indicated by Amazon's own statements and the ongoing advancements in AI, suggests that such capabilities are on the horizon.

3. **Finance: The Autonomous Investment Manager.** Organizations like Wealthfront and Betterment have been using AI to manage investments for years, offering automated portfolio management based on user preferences and risk tolerance. These platforms use algorithms to allocate assets, rebalance portfolios, and optimize tax strategies. The next generation of AI agents aims to take this further by actively monitoring global markets, predicting trends, and adjusting portfolios in real-time. The use of AI in finance, including portfolio management and market prediction, is a growing field. For example, Rebellion Research, a company specializing in AI-driven investment strategies, claims to use machine learning to identify market opportunities.

4. **Creative Industries: AI as a Collaborator.** In 2023, the band **yacht** released an album titled Chain Tripping, which was created in collaboration with AI. The band used machine learning tools to analyze their previous work and generate new lyrics, melodies, and chord progressions. The AI served as a creative collaborator, providing ideas that the band then refined and integrated into their music. While the album received attention for its innovative approach, critical reception was mixed, with some praising its experimental nature and others noting the challenges of blending human creativity with AI-generated content. This project highlights how AI can serve as a tool for artists, expanding creative possibilities rather than replacing human expression.

The Technology Behind the Magic

So, how do these AI agents work? At their core, they rely on three key technologies:

1. **Large Language Models (LLMs)**: These are the brains of the operation, enabling agents to understand and generate human-like text, video, audio, and more. Models like Open AI's ChatGPT and Anthropic's Claude are already capable of complex reasoning and problem-solving.

2. **Reinforcement Learning**: This allows agents to learn from experience. For example, an AI agent managing a supply chain can experiment with different strategies, learn what works, and continuously improve its performance. Humans provide feedback - Human in The Loop (HITL) - directing Agentic AI toward more and better answers.

3. **Multi-Agent Systems**: This is where the real power lies. By enabling agents to communicate and collaborate, we can tackle problems that are too complex for any single agent. Think of it as a hive mind, where each agent contributes its unique expertise.

Why Now?

The rise of AI agents is not just a result of technological progress—it is also driven by economic and societal forces. Organizations are under pressure to do more with less, and

AI agents offer a way to automate tasks, reduce costs, and unlock new opportunities. At the same time, consumers are demanding more personalized and efficient services, which AI agents are uniquely positioned to provide.

But the most key factor is the democratization of AI. Thanks to cloud computing and open-source tools, even small organizations and startups can now build and deploy AI agents. This is simultaneously leveling the playing field and accelerating innovation.

New Business Opportunities

The rise of AI agents is leading to the creation of entirely new ways to create value. From hyper-personalized services to decentralized autonomous organizations, the opportunities are vast and transformative. Let us explore some of the most promising examples.

1. Hyper-Personalized Services.

Imagine a world where every product, service, and interaction is tailored to your unique preferences, needs, and even emotions. AI agents are making this possible by analyzing vast amounts of data and delivering experiences that feel almost magical.

In healthcare organizations such as Vida Health are using AI agents to provide personalized wellness plans. These agents analyze your health data, from fitness trackers to medical records, and offer tailored advice on everything from diet to exercise to mental health.

In a study published in the Journal of Medical Internet Research Diabetes, participants with type 2 diabetes enrolled in Vida's virtual diabetes management program experienced clinically significant reductions in Hemoglobin A1c (HbA1c) levels after four months. Additionally, the Validation Institute confirmed that Vida's program leads to meaningful reductions in blood glucose levels, with high-risk participants seeing an average HbA1c reduction of 1.44 points.

In the education sector agents are already acting as the perfect tutor. AI agents are revolutionizing education by adapting to each student's learning style. Squirrel AI, a Chinese edtech company, uses AI tutors that identify gaps in a student's knowledge and deliver customized lessons.

In a study comparing the effectiveness of Squirrel AI's system to traditional classroom instruction, students using the AI tutor demonstrated a significant improvement in test scores, with an average increase of 5.4 points, compared to a 0.7-point increase in the traditional instruction group. It is not just about teaching—it is about teaching and educating better than before.

In retail, personal shopper company Stitch Fix, an online styling service, uses AI agents to analyze customer preferences and curate personalized clothing selections. The AI does not just look at your past purchases—it considers your style, budget, and even the weather in your area.

The result? A shopping experience that feels like it was designed just for you.

2. Automated Customer Support

Customer support is often a bottleneck for organizations, but AI agents are changing the game. These systems can manage complex queries, troubleshoot issues, and even escalate problems to human agents when necessary.

For example, Zendesk has integrated AI agents into its customer support platform, allowing organizations to automate rapidly. According to Zendesk, their AI features can automate up to 80% of support requests, leading to a three-fold increase in immediate, automated resolutions.

This contributes to a 30% decrease in resolution times and helps agents be at least 10% more productive, improving customer and contact center experience in the process.

3. Compound Systems for Complex Issues

Some problems are too complex for a single AI agent to manage. That is where compound systems come into play. For example, a banking customer might contact support with a multi-part issue involving fraud detection, account management, and loan applications. A network of AI agents can collaborate to resolve the issue seamlessly, with each agent specializing in a different area.

Intelligent process automation AI Agents are taking automation to the next level by managing entire workflows, not just individual tasks. This is especially valuable in industries like manufacturing, logistics, and finance.

Organizations like [Flexport](#) are using AI agents to manage and optimize their supply chains. These agents analyze data from suppliers, shipping organizations, and customers to optimize routes, reduce costs, and prevent delays.

AI agents are also transforming finance, often acting as autonomous CFOs. Pilot, a startup that provides bookkeeping services, uses AI to automate tasks like invoicing, payroll, and tax preparation.

The AI does not just crunch numbers—it identifies trends, flags anomalies, and even suggests ways to improve cash flow. It is like having a CFO who works 24/7.

4. AI-Driven Creativity and Content Creation

AI agents are not just logical; and they are creative. From writing music to designing logos, these systems are opening new possibilities for artists, marketers, and entrepreneurs.

For example, OpenAI's Jukebox is an AI agent that can generate original music in a wide variety of styles. In one experiment, a musician used a Jukebox to create a song in the style of David Bowie. The result was so convincing that it sparked a debate about the nature of creativity and authorship.

Organizations like Jasper.ai are using AI agents to generate and copywrite marketing copy. These agents can write blog posts, social media updates, and even ad campaigns. In one case, a small business used Jasper to create a month's worth of content in just two days, freeing up time to focus on strategy and customer engagement.

5. Smart Cities and Infrastructure

AI agents are transforming the way we manage cities, making them more efficient, sustainable, and liveable. For example, in Singapore, AI agents are used to optimize traffic flow in real-time. Agents analyze data from sensors, cameras, and GPS devices to autonomously adjust traffic lights, predict congestion, and even reroute public transportation to optimize traffic flow.

The result? A 15% reduction in travel time and a 20% drop in harmful emissions.

AI Agents are also being used to manage energy grids. In California, Grid4C uses AI to predict energy demand and adjust supply accordingly. This not only reduces costs but also helps integrate renewable energy sources like solar and wind.

6. Decentralized Autonomous Organizations (DAOs)

DAOs are organizations run by smart contracts and AI agents, with little to no human intervention. These entities are already being used for everything from investment funds to online communities.

In 2016, a group of developers launched the DAO, a decentralized investment fund managed by AI agents. While the project ultimately failed due to a security breach, it demonstrated the potential of AI-driven organizations. Today, newer DAOs are learning from these mistakes and building more robust systems.

7. AI-Powered Research and Development

AI agents are accelerating scientific discovery by simulating experiments, analyzing data, and generating hypotheses.

Drug discovery organizations like Insilico Medicine are using AI agents to identify potential drug candidates. In one case, an AI Agent discovered a new molecule for treating fibrosis in just 21 days—a process that would normally take years.

AI Agents are also being used to design new materials. For example, researchers at MIT are leveraging AI-powered techniques to discover a new type of battery electrolyte that could significantly improve energy storage.

8. Dynamic Pricing and Market Optimization

AI Agents are revolutionizing pricing strategies by analyzing market trends, competitor behavior, and consumer demand. For example, Uber uses real-time data analysis leveraging AI to adjust prices in real-time based on demand i.e., Uber Surge Pricing. This not only maximizes driver revenue but also ensures that drivers are available when and where they are needed most.

Amazon utilizes AI-driven dynamic pricing to continuously monitor competitors' prices and adjust their own accordingly. This creates a dynamic marketplace where prices are always optimized for both buyers and sellers.

9. AI-Enhanced Cybersecurity

AI agents are making cybersecurity more proactive and effective by detecting threats before they can cause harm. For example, Darktrace uses AI agents to monitor network traffic and identify unusual patterns. In one case, an AI agent detected a ransomware attack in its initial stages and neutralized it before any data was compromised.

10. Virtual Companions and Assistants

AI agents are becoming more than just tools; and they are becoming empathetic companions. For instance, Replika is an AI agent designed to provide emotional support and companionship. Users report feeling less lonely and more understood after interacting with their Replika.

Similarly, ElliQ is an AI Agent designed for seniors. It reminds them to take their medication, suggests activities, and even engages in conversation. Studies have demonstrated its effectiveness in reducing feelings of loneliness among older adults. For instance, a pilot program by the New York State Office for the Aging (NYSOFA) reported a 95% reduction in loneliness among participants using ElliQ.

Emerging Business Models

The rise of AI agents is enabling new ways of doing business. From subscription-based AI services to decentralized autonomous organizations, the business models of the future are being shaped by the capabilities of AI Agents. Let us explore some of the most promising models.

1. AI-as-a-Service (AIaaS)

Why build your own AI Agents when you can rent them? AIaaS platforms allow organizations to access advanced AI capabilities without the need for in-house expertise or infrastructure.

OpenAI's API allows developers to integrate GPT-4 and other AI models into their applications. For example, Copy.ai uses OpenAI's API to offer AI-powered copywriting tools to marketers. Organizations pay based on usage, making it affordable for startups and enterprises alike.

Similarly, Amazon's SageMaker platform provides pre-built algorithms and frameworks for tasks like data analysis, fraud detection, and natural language processing. Organizations like Intuit use SageMaker to enhance their financial software with AI-driven insights.

2. Outcome-Based Pricing

Instead of charging for time or resources, some organizations are using AI agents to deliver measurable results—and charging based on those outcomes. For example, Virta Health, a company specializing in diabetes reversal and metabolic health, uses a value-based pricing model.

Virta charges employers and insurers based on measurable outcomes, such as reduced healthcare costs and improved patient health metrics. If their AI-driven coaching platform helps patients avoid costly complications like hospital visits, Virta shares in the savings. This aligns incentives between the provider and the customer, ensuring that the AI agent is focused on delivering real, measurable value.

AI-driven marketing platforms are increasingly adopting performance-based pricing models, where customers pay based on the number of qualified leads or conversions generated. For example, [AdRoll](#) offers a pay-per-lead model for its AI-powered advertising platform, aligning incentives between the provider and the customer. This ensures that the AI Agent is focused on delivering real value, as the platform only gets paid when it produces measurable results. Such models are particularly appealing to organizations looking to minimize risk and maximize ROI in their marketing efforts.

3. AI Agent Marketplaces

Imagine an App Store but for AI Agents. These marketplaces allow developers to create and sell specialized agents while organizations can assemble compound systems tailored to their needs.

[Hugging Face](#) hosts thousands of AI models that can be combined to create custom solutions. For example, a retailer might use one agent for customer sentiment analysis and another for inventory management, building a more comprehensive AI-powered system.

Organizations like Microsoft are building ecosystems where AI agents from different providers can work together, creating AI Agent Ecosystems. For example, an AI agent for scheduling meetings might integrate with another agent for email management, creating a smooth workflow.

4. Subscription-Based AI Agents

Recurring revenue models are becoming increasingly popular for AI services, offering predictable costs for organizations and steady income for providers. For instance, Grammarly's AI-powered writing assistant is available on a subscription basis, with plans for individuals, teams, and enterprises. Users pay a monthly fee for access to advanced features like tone detection and plagiarism checking. Similarly, Calendly uses AI to optimize scheduling, reducing the back-and-forth of setting up meetings. Its subscription model makes it easy for organizations to scale as their needs grow.

5. Data Monetization via AI Agents

Many organizations are now using AI agents to analyze their data and sell insights to third parties. For example, Walmart uses AI Agents to analyze customer behavior and sell insights to suppliers to garner customer insight. For example, a snack manufacturer might use this data to optimize product placement and pricing.

6. AI-Enhanced Crowdsourcing

Combining human intelligence with AI-powered tools can solve complex problems more efficiently. For instance, Kaggle leverages AI-powered tools and features to assist participants in data science competitions. These tools include AutoML capabilities for model training and evaluation, as well as a collaborative environment where participants can share code and learn from each other's AI-driven approaches.

8. AI-Powered Licensing and IP

Licensing AI-generated outputs is becoming a lucrative business model. Organizations like Artbreeder allow users to create and license AI-generated art. This opens new revenue streams for artists and designers.

9. Ethical AI Consulting

As AI adoption grows, so does the need for ethical oversight. Firms like O'Neil Risk Consulting & Algorithmic Auditing (ORCAA) help organizations ensure their AI systems are fair, transparent, and compliant with regulations.

Challenges and Considerations

While the opportunities are vast, the rise of AI Agents also brings about challenges. Below are some key considerations for organizations and policymakers:

1. **Ethical Concerns:**

   - **Bias and Fairness**: AI Agents can perpetuate biases present in their training data. For example, a hiring AI might favor certain demographics over others. Addressing this requires rigorous testing and ongoing monitoring.

   - **Transparency and Accountability**: AI Agents often operate as "black boxes," making it difficult to understand their decision-making processes. This lack of transparency can lead to mistrust and legal challenges.

2. **Regulatory and Legal Challenges:**

   - **Data Privacy**: AI Agents rely on vast amounts of data, raising concerns about privacy and consent. Regulations like GDPR and CCPA dictate how organizations can legally collect and use data.

   - **Liability**: Who is responsible when an AI Agent makes a mistake? This question is still largely unanswered, creating uncertainty for organizations.

3. **Scalability and Interoperability:**

   - **Integration Challenges:** AI Agents from different providers may not work well together, limiting their effectiveness. Standardization efforts are needed to ensure interoperability.

- **Resource Constraints:** While cloud computing has made AI more accessible, training and deploying advanced agents still require significant and costly computing resources.

4. Job Displacement and Economic Impact:

- **The Future of Work**: AI Agents are automating tasks traditionally performed by humans, raising concerns about job displacement. However, they also create new roles in AI development, oversight, and maintenance.

- **Economic Inequality**: The benefits of AI Agents may not be evenly distributed, exacerbating existing inequalities. Policymakers and organizations must work to ensure inclusive growth and digital inclusion.

5. Security Risks:

- **Adversarial Attacks:** AI Agents are vulnerable to attacks that manipulate their behavior. For example, an attacker might feed an AI agent misleading data to cause it to make incorrect decisions.

- **Data Breaches:** The data used to train and operate AI Agents is a valuable target for hackers. Robust security measures are essential to protect this information.

Conclusion

The rise of AI Agents and compound Agentic AI systems is transforming the business landscape, creating opportunities that were unimaginable just a few years ago. From hyper-personalized services to decentralized autonomous organizations, the possibilities are endless. But with great power comes great responsibility. Organizations must navigate ethical, regulatory, and technical challenges to harness the full potential of these technologies.

As we move forward, one thing is clear: the future belongs to those who can adapt, innovate, and collaborate—not just with humans but with the intelligent agents that are becoming our partners in progress.

References

- AutoGPT - https://autogpt.net/everything-you-need-to-know-about-the-autogpt-platform/

- AlphaFold - https://deepmind.google/discover/blog/alphafold-using-ai-for-scientific-discovery-2020/

- AlphaStar - https://deepmind.google/discover/blog/alphastar-mastering-the-real-time-strategy-game-starcraft-ii/

- Hippocratic AI - https://www.hippocraticai.com/

- Amazon statement - https://www.aboutamazon.in/news/devices/amazon-alexa-ai-innovations

- Wealthfront - https://www.wealthfront.com/

- Betterment - https://www.betterment.com/

- AI in finance - https://www.bcg.com/publications/2024/ai-next-wave-of-transformation

- Collaboration with AI - https://www.opb.org/article/2022/10/20/portland-band-yacht-experiments-with-artificial-intelligence-and-music/

- Medical Study - https://www.vida.com/news/vida-healths-virtual-diabetes-program-achieves-meaningful-clinical-outcomes-in-reducing-hba1c/

- And the Validation Institute confirmed - https://www.vida.com/news/validation-institute-confirms-vida-healths-diabetes-management-program-shows-meaningful-outcomes-and-cost-savings/

- Study AI-Based Adaptive Learning Systems - https://arxiv.org/abs/1901.10268

- Stitch Fix - https://newsroom.stitchfix.com/blog/how-were-revolutionizing-personal-styling-with-generative-ai/

- Zendesk - https://www.zendesk.com/in/service/

- According to Zendesk - https://www.prnewswire.com/news-releases/zendesk-unveils-the-industrys-most-complete-service-solution-for-the-ai-era-302117280.html

- Flexport - https://www.freethink.com/robots-ai/generative-ai-shipping

- A security breach - https://medium.com/@syedhasnaatabbas/the-dao-hack-and-its-aftermath-lessons-learned-in-decentralized-security-e5e2df0d1174

- DAOs - https://www.aragon.org/how-to/the-future-of-daos-is-powered-by-ai

- Insilico Medicine - https://www.forbes.com/sites/alexknapp/2019/09/02/this-startup-used-ai-to-design-a-drug-in-21-days/

- Battery Researcher at MIT - https://www.technologyreview.com/2023/10/12/1081502/ai-battery-research

- Surge Pricing - https://www.uber.com/us/en/marketplace/pricing/surge-pricing/

- AI-driven dynamic pricing - https://aws.amazon.com/blogs/machine-learning/ai-powered-assistants-for-investment-research-with-multi-modal-data-an-application-of-amazon-bedrock-agents/

- Darktrace - https://darktrace.com/cyber-ai

- Replika - https://replika.com/

- ElliQ - https://elliq.com/

- Loneliness pilot program - https://aging.ny.gov/news/nysofas-rollout-ai-companion-robot-elliq-shows-95-reduction-loneliness

- Copy.ai - http://copy.ai

- SageMaker - https://aws.amazon.com/sagemaker/

- Intuit - https://aws.amazon.com/solutions/case-studies/intuit-reinvent/

- Virta Health - https://www.virtahealth.com/

- Value-based pricing model - https://www.businesswire.com/news/home/20181114005310/en/Virta-Health-Puts-100-of-Fees-at-Risk-with-Announcement-of-New-Pricing-Structure#:~:text=Virta%20Health%20introduces%20a%20new%20pricing%20structure,majority%20of%20payment%20to%20diabetes%20reversal%20outcomes.

- AdRoll - https://www.adroll.com/pricing

- Hugging Face - https://huggingface.co/docs/hub/en/models-the-hub

- Copilot Ecosystems - https://www.microsoft.com/en-us/microsoft-copilot/organizations/

- Grammarly AI-powered writing assistant - https://www.grammarly.com/ai

- Calendly - https://calendly.com/

- Analyse customer behavior and sell insights to suppliers - https://corporate.walmart.com/news/2024/04/17/creating-more-opportunities-for-data-driven-supplier-growth-at-walmart

- Kaggle - https://www.kaggle.com/

- Artbreeder - https://www.artbreeder.com/

- O'Neil Risk Consulting & Algorithmic Auditing - https://orcaarisk.com/

Chapter 9

The Agentic AI Ecosystem:
Market Trends, Key Players, and Future Outlook

9

The Agentic AI Ecosystem: Market Trends, Key Players, and Future Outlook

In today's era, AI agents have emerged as one of the most intriguing and transformative technological developments. These systems—ranging from conversational virtual assistants to sophisticated autonomous decision-makers—are reshaping how organizations interact with customers, optimize internal processes, and even innovate new business models. What was once the domain of science fiction is now a tangible, market-driving reality. Over the past decade, advances in machine learning, natural language processing, and cloud computing have converged to give rise to AI Agents that are not only capable of understanding complex inputs but can also act on them in real-time. Whether it is scheduling meetings, providing customer support, or even analyzing large data sets for actionable insights, these agents are making it possible to automate tasks that previously required human intervention.

The pace of change is rapid, and the competitive advantage goes to those organizations that can integrate these agents into their strategic framework.

This article aims to provide a comprehensive description of the current AI Agent's market. We will explore what AI agents are, the core technologies that underpin them, and the ways in which they are deployed across various industries. In doing so, we will shed light on the offerings of major players, both tech giants and innovative startups, and the trends that are driving the market forward. Along the way, we will include engaging real-world case studies to illustrate how these agents are making a difference in everyday business operations.

For instance, consider Google's demonstration of Duplex, a system capable of conducting natural, human-like conversations to book appointments on behalf of users. Duplex was initially showcased as a standalone technology; its capabilities have been integrated into other Google Assistant features and services. What might have seemed like sci-fi is now a concrete example of how AI Agents can be leveraged to manage everyday tasks.

Similarly, IBM Watson's deployment in healthcare diagnostics has helped streamline processes and improve patient outcomes by providing physicians with rapid, data-driven insights. These examples underscore the practical implications of AI agent technology.

What are AI Agents?

Simply put, an AI agent is a software system that perceives its environment, processes information and acts in ways that optimize the achievement of specific goals. This definition shows the wide range of functionalities AI agents possess, from providing immediate customer support to complex decision-making processes over extended periods. Unlike basic automated scripts or rule-based chatbots, modern AI agents utilize machine learning to continuously refine their responses, learning from past interactions to adapt their strategies and even anticipate user needs in a manner reminiscent of human intuition.

These agents manifest in various forms. Some, like Apple's Siri, Amazon's Alexa, and Google Assistant, are designed for direct human-machine interaction, enhancing consumer engagement and boosting personal productivity. Others operate with a higher degree of independence in enterprise or industrial settings, where they automate tasks such as data entry, scheduling, or even entire back-office operations through robotic process automation. There are also specialized AI agents tailored to the unique demands of industries such as healthcare and finance; for example, in healthcare, they might analyze patient data to support diagnostics, while in finance, they monitor transactions to detect anomalies and prevent fraud.

Underpinning these sophisticated systems are several key technologies. Machine learning lies at the core, enabling agents to improve decision-making over time by processing vast amounts of data using various learning techniques. Natural language processing (NLP) empowers these agents to understand, generate, and respond to human language with increasing fluency, which is a critical capability for developing conversational interfaces. Additionally, the scalability offered by cloud computing is essential for managing large data volumes and supporting real-time interactions, while integration with the Internet of Things (IoT) and other external systems allows AI agents to access comprehensive datasets, enhancing their decision-making capabilities. For instance, in smart factories, AI agents can synthesize sensor data from machinery to predict maintenance needs and prevent costly downtime.

The practical applications of AI agents are both diverse and impactful. In customer service, AI-powered chatbots manage routine inquiries, liberating human agents to tackle more complex issues.

IBM Watson, for example, has been implemented in retail settings to deliver precise, context-aware responses. In the field of process automation, these agents streamline tasks such as scheduling, data entry, and logistics, reducing errors and boosting overall efficiency.

Beyond automation, AI agents serve as powerful decision-support tools by analyzing large datasets in real-time to provide actionable insights—a capability that has significantly improved diagnostic accuracy in healthcare. In addition, by personalizing user interactions based on browsing and purchasing behaviors, virtual assistants in e-commerce transform the customer experience and drive increased engagement.

These examples illustrate the remarkable flexibility of AI agents. Their capacity to be finely tuned to the specific needs of an organization has enabled a level of operational efficiency and innovation that was unimaginable just a decade ago.

Market Overview and Trends

According to MarketsandMarkets, the global AI market is projected to grow from $214.6 billion in 2024 to $1339.1 billion in 2030 at a Compound Annual Growth Rate (CAGR) of around 35.7% during the forecast period. This growth is reflective of both increased investment in AI research and the accelerating adoption of AI-driven solutions across industries. Several key trends are shaping the evolution of the AI agent market:

1. **Deep Personalization and Contextual Understanding.** AI agents are becoming better at understanding the context of interactions, leading to highly personalized experiences. Advances in NLP and contextual machine learning have enabled agents to interpret nuanced human communications, thereby tailoring responses based on a user's history and preferences.

2. **Integration with Broader Ecosystems.** Modern AI agents are rarely standalone systems. They are increasingly embedded within larger digital ecosystems that include IoT devices, enterprise resource planning (ERP) systems, and data analytics platforms.

3. **Edge Computing and Real-Time Processing.** With the rise of edge computing, AI agents are moving closer to the data source, reducing latency and improving real-time responsiveness. This is particularly important in applications such as autonomous vehicles and industrial automation, where split-second decisions are critical.

4. **Ethical and Regulatory Considerations.** As the deployment of AI agents becomes ubiquitous, issues related to data privacy, algorithmic bias, and regulatory compliance are coming to the forefront. Organizations must navigate a complex landscape of legal and ethical

guidelines while ensuring that their AI systems remain transparent and accountable.

Challenges and Opportunities

Despite the significant potential, the market for AI agents is not without its challenges:

- **Data Quality and Integration.** The effectiveness of an AI agent is fundamentally linked to the quality of data it is trained on and the systems it integrates with. Inconsistent data formats, siloed information, and legacy IT infrastructures can all pose significant hurdles to seamless integration and optimal performance.

- **Trust and Adoption.** For many organizations, the transition from human-led processes to automated systems involves not only technical challenges but also cultural and psychological ones. Building trust in AI agents—ensuring that decision-makers and end users alike are confident in the technology—is a critical step for widespread adoption.

- **Scalability and Maintenance.** As AI agents are deployed at scale, maintaining their performance and updating them to cope with evolving business requirements becomes increasingly complex. Enterprises must invest in robust monitoring and maintenance frameworks to ensure that their AI systems continue to deliver value over time.

On the opportunity side, however, the potential benefits are considerable. By automating routine tasks, AI agents free up human capital for higher-value activities such as strategic decision-making and innovation. Moreover, the data insights generated by these agents can lead to improved operational efficiencies, more personalized customer interactions, and, ultimately, a stronger competitive edge.

A striking example of this opportunity is seen in the healthcare sector. Institutions such as the Mayo Clinic have begun leveraging AI-driven diagnostic tools to sift through vast amounts of medical data, thereby enhancing the accuracy and speed of diagnoses. Such real-world implementations not only validate the technology but also set the stage for broader adoption across industries that are eager to tap into the transformative power of AI agents.

Key Players in the AI Agents Market

The competitive landscape for AI agents is defined by a mix of established tech giants, innovative startups, and regional players. In this section, we provide a detailed look at the key players who are shaping the market, highlighting their offerings and strategic differentiators.

Tech Giants and Established Corporations

Google. Google has established itself as a front-runner in the AI agent space. Its flagship offerings include Google Assistant, a widely used virtual assistant available on smartphones, smart speakers, and various other devices, and Dialogflow, a platform that enables developers to build conversational interfaces for applications ranging from customer support to IoT device management. Google's strategy centers on leveraging its extensive data resources and cloud infrastructures and integrating its AI agents into a broader ecosystem—including Google Cloud and Android—to create a network effect that drives adoption across both consumer and enterprise markets.

Microsoft. Microsoft's strategic investments in AI and cloud computing have firmly established it as a leader in enterprise AI solutions, with offerings that seamlessly integrate into its expansive suite of productivity and business tools. Key products include Azure Bot Services, a robust framework for building and deploying intelligent bots that work across various Microsoft services and third-party applications, and Cortana, which has evolved from a consumer-facing assistant into an enterprise productivity tool embedded within Microsoft 365 to assist with scheduling, reminders, and task management.

Emphasizing deep integration with its ecosystem, spanning Office 365, Azure, and Dynamics 365, Microsoft streamlines workflows, enhances productivity, and ensures that AI-driven insights are immediately actionable.

Additionally, with significant stakes in OpenAI and strategic acquisitions such as GitHub and investments in tools like Visual Studio Code, Microsoft has effectively captured both the developer and enterprise software markets.

Amazon. Amazon's approach to AI agents is characterized by a dual focus on consumer convenience and enterprise efficiency, driven by extensive investments that have produced solutions that are both robust and widely accessible. Key offerings include Alexa, a virtual assistant powering smart speakers, home automation systems, and a variety of consumer devices, alongside AWS AI Services, a suite of AI and machine learning tools that enable organizations to integrate AI agents. Alexa's widespread adoption in smart home devices has made it a household name, while AWS-powered AI solutions are increasingly deployed in sectors such as logistics and retail.

Leveraging its deep legacy in data processing, IBM delivers robust, industry-specific solutions by concentrating on high-value enterprise applications such as healthcare diagnostics and financial risk management, thereby positioning Watson as a trusted partner in navigating complex, data-driven challenges.

The transformative impact of IBM Watson is evident in its widespread adoption in healthcare, where hospitals and research institutions utilize the platform to assist in diagnosing diseases, managing patient data, and identifying potential treatment pathways, with partnerships with leading institutions like Mayo Clinic reinforcing IBM's reputation as a leader in applying AI to solve critical problems.

Pegasystems has been a force in the AI agent landscape for quite some time, leveraging its platform to unify intelligent automation, real-time decision-making, and enterprise-grade governance. Unlike competitors focused on broad consumer-facing applications, Pega's strategy centers on embedding AI deeply into business workflows, enabling organizations to automate complex processes while maintaining compliance and adaptability. The Pega Platform combines robotic process automation (RPA), business process management (BPM), and machine learning to create end-to-end workflows that adapt to real-time data.

For example, Pega Process AI uses predictive analytics to pre-empt service-level agreement (SLA) breaches, automatically rerouting tasks to optimize outcomes. By integrating AI agents with its low-code platform, Pega empowers organizations to orchestrate dynamic customer experiences, optimize operational efficiency, and scale AI-driven solutions across industries.

A key differentiator for Pega is its emphasis on responsible AI, particularly through the Pega Agent Experience™ (AgentX). Announced in February 2025, AgentX tackles the industry-wide challenge of unreliable AI agents by embedding governance directly into workflows. While Microsoft's Azure Bot Services and Google's Dialogflow offer flexibility, they often lack built-in mechanisms to prevent agents from generating inconsistent or non-compliant outputs. Pega AgentX transforms workflows into "agentic orchestration engines," dynamically guiding AI agents to complete tasks while invoking secondary agents for validation. This layered governance model mitigates risks associated with generative AI, making Pega a preferred choice for highly regulated sectors like finance and healthcare.

Innovative Startups and Niche Players

While the tech giants dominate in scale and reach, the market is also enriched by innovative startups that bring niche, disruptive solutions to specific problems. Perplexity AI, with its focus on conversational search and knowledge retrieval, leverages large language models to provide users with direct answers and source citations rather than just a list of links. This approach represents a shift towards more interactive and informative search experiences, potentially disrupting traditional search paradigms. Their focus on accuracy and transparency, by providing source information, differentiates them within the crowded AI landscape.

Regional Leaders and Differences

The global nature of the AI agents market means that regional dynamics also play a significant role in shaping product offerings and adoption rates:

European Market:

European organizations have long emphasized data privacy and regulatory compliance, driven by stringent local laws such as the GDPR. Recently, however, the European landscape has evolved significantly. In 2024-2025, initiatives like the Digital Europe Programme and the forthcoming EU AI Act have spurred both regulatory rigor and innovation. These efforts aim to foster a unified digital market that not only upholds data security and transparency but also accelerates investment in next-generation AI technologies. As a result, European firms are emerging as competitive players on the global stage, balancing robust regulatory standards with an increasing focus on technological advancement.

Asian Market:

In contrast, the Asian market, particularly in countries like China and Japan, is known for its rapid adoption and innovation in consumer-facing AI. Traditionally dominated by established players such as Baidu and Alibaba, the region is now witnessing a seismic shift. DeepSeek, a disruptive innovator, is challenging the established hegemony of global giants like OpenAI, Microsoft, and Nvidia. By leveraging localized strategies and offering high-performance, cost-effective AI solutions, DeepSeek is reshaping competitive dynamics and signaling that innovation in Asia is as much about agility and disruption as it is about scale.

North American Dominance:

North America continues to be a hotbed for AI innovation, propelled by cutting-edge research institutions, robust venture capital, and a culture steeped in technological experimentation. Our region is not just participating in but actively leading the global AI arms race, driving breakthroughs across diverse sectors. This leadership is reinforced by strategic geopolitical measures; recent U.S. export controls have effectively restricted access to critical semiconductor and chip technologies for competitors in China and India. These sanctions underscore North America's commitment to maintaining a competitive edge in advanced AI hardware, further cementing its dominant position in the global landscape.

Real-World Impact:

Regional preferences can be seen in the deployment of AI agents tailored to local market needs. For example, European banks have been early adopters of AI-driven fraud detection systems that comply with local data protection laws, while Asian e-commerce platforms leverage highly localized virtual assistants to enhance user engagement and conversion rates.

Case Studies and Real-World Applications

To move beyond abstract market dynamics, it is critical to examine how AI agents are actively transforming business operations across diverse industries. This section explores real-world deployments, both at the enterprise level and within specific industries, shedding light on practical outcomes, measurable benefits, and the lessons learned from early adopters.

Enterprise Case Studies

Large organizations have been quick to integrate AI agents into core workflows, leveraging automation to enhance efficiency and support data-driven decision-making.

Enhancing Customer Support in Retail. A prime example is the implementation of AI-driven chatbots by global retailers. Consider how Sephora employs conversational agents to offer personalized product recommendations, beauty tips, and appointment scheduling. By integrating AI into its mobile app and website, Sephora has not only improved customer engagement but also reduced the load on human support teams.

Streamlining Back-Office Operations. UiPath has been at the forefront of deploying autonomous software agents to manage repetitive tasks such as invoice processing and data reconciliation. Large financial institutions have integrated these agents to automate complex workflows, resulting in significant reductions in processing time and error rates. For instance, one global bank reported a decrease in manual processing costs by nearly 40% after implementing UiPath's RPA solutions, freeing up staff to focus on strategic tasks.

Advancing Diagnostic Accuracy in Healthcare. Healthcare institutions have found that AI agents can dramatically improve both efficiency and accuracy in patient care. Aidoc, for example, has deployed AI algorithms in radiology departments to analyze CT scans and X-ray images. This real-time analysis assists radiologists in quickly identifying abnormalities, thereby accelerating the diagnostic process and reducing the likelihood of human error.

Industry-Specific Examples

Different sectors have harnessed AI agents to address unique challenges, and the impact of these applications has been both transformative and measurable.

Financial Services. In finance, AI agents are revolutionizing risk management and fraud detection. One notable case is the adoption of AI-driven contract analysis systems by JP Morgan Chase. Their COiN (Contract Intelligence) platform leverages machine learning to review and interpret complex legal documents, reducing what once took thousands of hours of manual labor into mere seconds. The successful deployment of such systems not only minimizes risk but also accelerates decision-making processes.

Manufacturing and Smart Factories. In industrial settings, AI agents are used to optimize production lines and predict equipment failures. In a smart factory scenario, sensor data is continuously monitored by AI systems that analyze operational patterns to forecast maintenance needs. This proactive approach, demonstrated by organizations such as Siemens, helps prevent unplanned downtime and maximizes production efficiency.

Travel and Hospitality. Airlines and hotels have also turned to AI agents to refine customer experience and operational efficiency. For instance, AI-powered virtual assistants can be used to manage bookings, provide real-time travel updates, and resolve common inquiries.

Lessons Learned and Best Practices

Real-world deployments of AI agents underscore several best practices and critical lessons:

- **Data Quality is Paramount.** The efficacy of an AI agent hinges on the quality and consistency of the underlying data. Enterprises that invest in robust data governance and integration frameworks tend to see more substantial returns from AI implementations.

- **Incremental Integration Pays Off.** Rather than a "big bang" approach, successful organizations often introduce AI agents in stages. Starting with less critical tasks and gradually expanding the scope allows teams to build confidence in the technology while mitigating risk.

- **Transparency and User Trust.** Ensuring that AI-driven decisions are explainable is crucial for both regulatory compliance and user acceptance. Efforts toward developing explainable AI have been instrumental in gaining buy-in from stakeholders, particularly in sectors like healthcare and finance.

- **Continuous Improvement.** The dynamic nature of business processes means that AI agents require regular updates and performance monitoring. Establishing feedback loops and robust maintenance protocols helps ensure that AI systems continue to meet evolving business needs.

Competitive Landscape and Strategic Insights

Beyond individual deployments, the overall competitive dynamics within the AI agents market provide valuable insights into how technological differentiation and strategic positioning are shaping the industry's evolution. This section dissects how market leaders are differentiating themselves, the role of mergers and strategic collaborations, and the future competitive strategies likely to redefine the landscape.

Market Positioning and Differentiators

In a market crowded with both tech giants and agile startups, differentiation is key. Organizations are carving out unique positions based on factors such as specialization, scalability, and integration capabilities.

- **Specialization vs. Generalization.** While some players focus on broad, versatile platforms (e.g., Google Assistant, Microsoft's Azure Bot Services), others target niche applications with specialized solutions. For instance, Aidoc focuses exclusively on medical imaging analysis, allowing it to fine-tune its algorithms for healthcare settings. This specialization offers a competitive edge in markets where domain expertise is critical.

- **Integration Capabilities.** The ability to seamlessly integrate with existing IT ecosystems is a major differentiator. Organizations that provide robust APIs and support for hybrid deployment models (both cloud and on-premises) are better positioned to meet the diverse needs of enterprises. Google Cloud's DialogFlow and Microsoft's Azure Bot Services exemplify platforms that emphasize integration and scalability—two features that are highly valued in enterprise environments.

- **Data Security and Compliance.** In industries like finance and healthcare, data security is non-negotiable. Firms that invest in encryption, access controls, and compliance with regulatory frameworks (such as GDPR and HIPAA) not only reduce risk but also build trust among their clientele. IBM Watson's healthcare solutions, for example, have been carefully tailored to meet stringent data protection requirements, helping to secure its position in sensitive markets.

Mergers, Acquisitions, and Collaborations

The competitive dynamics of the AI agent's market are further shaped by strategic mergers, acquisitions, and collaborations. These moves often accelerate innovation and broaden market reach:

- **Consolidation for Scale.** Major technology organizations are increasingly acquiring smaller, specialized firms to integrate cutting-edge AI capabilities into their broader ecosystems. These acquisitions not only expand the technological portfolio of the acquirers but also accelerate time-to-market for innovative solutions. The integration of niche startups into platforms like AWS or Microsoft Azure allows for rapid scalability and a more comprehensive service offering.

- **Collaborative Ecosystems.** Partnerships between tech giants and industry-specific players are also driving innovation. For example, collaborations between IBM and leading healthcare institutions have resulted in tailor-made AI solutions that address real-world clinical challenges.

- **Strategic partnerships** allow organizations to combine technical prowess with domain expertise, resulting in products that are both technically advanced and highly relevant to end users.

- **Open-Source and Community-Driven Innovation.** The rise of open-source platforms has also played a role in shaping competitive dynamics. Open-source AI frameworks enable smaller players and even large enterprises to contribute to and benefit from a shared pool of knowledge, accelerating overall innovation within the market.

Future Competitive Strategies

Looking ahead, several trends and strategies are likely to influence the competitive landscape of AI agents:

- **Enhanced Personalization and Context Awareness.** Future AI agents will be designed to provide even more personalized experiences, leveraging advances in contextual understanding and predictive analytics.

- **Organizations that invest in these** areas are likely to lead the market by delivering solutions that adapt seamlessly to user needs and business contexts.

- **Focus on Explainable AI.** As regulatory pressures mount and end-user trust becomes paramount, the ability to explain AI-driven decisions will become a significant competitive differentiator. Firms that can strike the right balance between algorithmic complexity and interpretability will have a distinct advantage in industries where transparency is essential.

- **Edge Computing and Decentralized Processing.** With the increasing importance of real-time decision-making, particularly in sectors like autonomous vehicles and industrial automation, competitive strategies will pivot towards integrating edge computing capabilities. AI agents that process data locally while remaining connected to centralized learning systems will be better equipped to manage latency-sensitive tasks and complex operational scenarios.

- **Sustainability and Ethical AI.** Finally, the next phase of competition may well be defined by an organization's commitment to sustainable and ethical AI practices.

Organizations that proactively address issues of bias, privacy, and environmental impact are not only likely to earn regulatory favor but also to build a loyal customer base in an increasingly conscientious market.

In summary, the competitive landscape of AI agents is characterized by a blend of technological differentiation, strategic consolidation, and forward-thinking innovation. By focusing on integration, specialization, and ethical practices, market leaders are positioning themselves to capitalize on the explosive growth of AI-driven automation—a trend that promises to reshape industries for years to come.

Outlook and Market Predictions

As the AI agents market continues its rapid evolution, a confluence of technological advances, shifting business models, and regulatory considerations is poised to reshape the landscape. In this section, we examine the trends and predictions that will define the next phase of AI agent development and deployment.

Technological Advancements on the Horizon

1. Enhanced Personalization and Context Awareness

The next generation of AI agents will move well beyond basic task automation. Advances in deep learning and contextual analytics are paving the way for systems that not only respond to explicit commands but also anticipate user needs. As natural language processing (NLP) and computer vision technologies improve, AI agents will be better equipped to interpret nuanced data, from tone in customer communications to subtle patterns in operational metrics. For example, imagine an AI agent that dynamically adjusts its recommendations based on real-time shifts in consumer behavior, much like how modern recommendation engines on platforms such as Netflix continuously refine suggestions based on viewer habits.

2. Edge Computing and Decentralized Processing

With the increasing demand for real-time decision-making, especially in critical industries like autonomous vehicles and industrial automation, edge computing is set to play a central role. AI agents integrated with edge computing capabilities can process data locally, significantly reducing latency and improving responsiveness. This trend is already visible in sectors like manufacturing, where systems that predict equipment maintenance using sensor data can prevent downtime and optimize resource allocation.

3. Integration with Emerging Technologies

The future will also see AI agents interfacing more seamlessly with other emerging technologies such as blockchain, augmented reality (AR), and 5G networks. These integrations will unlock new applications, from secure, decentralized data sharing to real-time, immersive customer interactions, that further extend the capabilities of AI agents. For instance, blockchain's immutable record-keeping could be used to enhance the trustworthiness of automated decision logs, an essential factor in regulated industries.

Evolving Business Models and Deployment Strategies

Hybrid Deployment Models

While cloud-based SaaS models currently dominate due to their scalability and ease of integration, there is a growing trend toward hybrid deployment models. These models combine the flexibility of the cloud with the enhanced security and customization offered by on-premises solutions. This evolution is particularly critical in industries with stringent data privacy regulations, such as finance and healthcare. As organizations seek to balance innovation with compliance, hybrid models will become the norm.

Shifts in Pricing and Value Delivery

The monetization strategies for AI agents are also expected to evolve. Beyond traditional subscription or pay-per-use models, we may see more value-based pricing structures that align costs with the measurable business outcomes that AI agents deliver. For example, rather than a flat fee, pricing might be tied to improvements in operational efficiency or revenue growth—mirroring trends in performance-based contracting seen in other high-tech sectors.

Broader Market Impacts and Competitive Dynamics

Increased Focus on Explainable AI

As AI agents take on more critical decision-making roles, the need for transparency and explainability will intensify. Regulatory bodies and end users alike are demanding systems that not only perform well but can also justify their actions in understandable terms. This requirement is driving investments in explainable AI (XAI), an area that seeks to bridge the gap between algorithmic complexity and human comprehension. Organizations that excel in providing clear, auditable insights into their AI systems will have a significant competitive edge, especially in highly regulated markets.

Regulatory and Ethical Considerations

The regulatory environment for AI is rapidly maturing, with new policies emerging worldwide to address issues such as data privacy, algorithmic bias, and accountability. In the coming years, we can expect more robust frameworks that will shape how AI agents are developed and deployed.

Organizations that proactively integrate ethical considerations into their AI strategies, not merely as an afterthought but as a core component, will be better positioned to navigate these challenges. The emphasis on ethical AI is likely to influence everything from product design to business strategy, ensuring that AI agents contribute positively to society and maintain public trust.

Competitive Consolidation and Innovation

Finally, the market is poised for further consolidation as established players continue to acquire innovative startups to bolster their AI portfolios. At the same time, open-source communities and collaborative ecosystems will play a crucial role in accelerating innovation.

As the boundaries between sectors blur, organizations that can offer flexible, interoperable solutions will be best equipped to capture emerging opportunities. This dynamic, where both large-scale consolidation and grassroots innovation coexist, promises to drive the next wave of transformative applications in AI agent technology.

Conclusion

The journey through the AI agents market reveals a landscape that is both dynamic and profoundly transformative. What began as experimental applications in consumer gadgets and enterprise systems has matured into a robust ecosystem characterized by diverse applications, strategic industry players, and rapidly evolving technological capabilities.

For organizations contemplating the integration of AI agents, the potential benefits are substantial. From automating routine processes to unlocking new levels of customer engagement and data-driven decision-making, AI agents offer a compelling value proposition. However, success in this arena requires more than just technological adoption. It calls for a strategic vision that aligns AI initiatives with broader business objectives and ethical considerations.

Enterprises that invest in robust data governance, foster a culture of continuous innovation, and maintain a clear focus on explainable and sustainable AI are likely to reap the rewards of this digital revolution. The AI agents' market is not static; it is an evolving frontier where today's investments lay the groundwork for tomorrow's competitive advantage.

As we stand on the cusp of the next wave of AI-driven transformation, the imperative for forward-thinking leaders is clear: embrace the potential of AI agents with both enthusiasm and a critical, strategic eye. Evaluate where automation can not only streamline operations but also serve as a catalyst for innovation and enhanced decision-making. As regulatory and ethical frameworks evolve, commit to developing AI solutions that are transparent, accountable, and aligned with the broader values of your organization.

References:

- https://research.google/blog/google-duplex-an-ai-system-for-accomplishing-real-world-tasks-over-the-phone/

- https://www.ibm.com/products/watsonx-assistant/healthcare

- https://www.siemens.com/global/en/products/automation/topic-areas/artificial-intelligence-in-industry/usecases/ai-based-predictive-maintenance.html

- https://www.aidoc.com/

- https://www.reuters.com/technology/artificial-intelligence/what-is-deepseek-why-is-it-disrupting-ai-sector-2025-01-27

- https://insights.sei.cmu.edu/blog/what-is-explainable-ai/

Chapter 10

Agentic AI Architecture:
From Low-Code Platforms to Full-Code Solutions

10

Agentic AI Architecture: From Low-Code Platforms to Full-Code Solutions

Imagine a factory in the 1800s. Workers manually operate looms until steam engines arrive, automating production. Fast-forward to today: the looms are business processes, and the steam engines are autonomous agents, AI systems that make decisions, act, and learn with minimal human oversight. AI agents are not sci-fi fantasies; they are already answering customer emails, qualifying sales leads, and optimizing supply chains without human guidance. Since agents seem to be much more capable of reasoning and action, in contrast to traditional software programs, it may well be said that they traverse the space between programmed instruction and emergent intelligence.

As expected, building these agents is not a simple, one-size-fits-all task. Their development spans a spectrum: on one end, low-code and no-code platforms provide accessible, rapid development environments that allow teams with limited programming expertise to create functional prototypes and solutions; on the other end, full-code solutions enable custom, high-performance applications built from the ground up.

Organizations choose their approach based on factors such as time-to-market, cost, available technical expertise, scalability needs, and the level of customization required. Whether leveraging low-code platforms for agility or full-code development for control and performance, understanding the trade-offs is essential for successfully integrating Agentic AI into any enterprise environment.

This article serves as a guide to navigating these trade-offs. We will analyze low-code, hybrid, and full-code approaches through real-world perspectives, cutting through the hype to focus on what truly delivers business results, not just what appears impressive.

Low-Code Agent Development

Low-code agent development platforms are analogous to IKEA furniture, providing pre-built components (e.g., APIs, workflows, templates). These platforms provide visual interfaces and drag-and-drop components that accelerate the prototyping and deployment process, making them ideal for organizations looking to implement AI solutions quickly.

One of the prominent tools in this space is Langchain, a framework designed to simplify the integration of language models (LLMs) into applications. Langchain streamlines complex tasks such as prompt engineering, response handling, and chaining multiple LLM calls to build coherent workflows. Similarly, LlamaIndex assists in managing and indexing large volumes of data, which is crucial for agents that rely on contextual information to generate accurate responses.

In addition to these frameworks, no-code platforms like Zapier and Make.com (formerly Integromat) provide extensive libraries of pre-built integrations. These platforms allow users to automate workflows by connecting various services—ranging from email and CRM systems to social media and e-commerce platforms—without writing a single line of code. By linking these integrations with LLM APIs from providers such as OpenAI, Anthropic, or Cohere, organizations can deploy agents that manage tasks like customer support, order processing, or content generation with relative ease.

A practical example of low-code agent deployment is a Customer Service Autoresponder. In this scenario, a business uses a low-code platform to connect its customer relationship management (CRM) system with an LLM API. When a customer inquiry is received, the agent quickly processes the query, identifies common questions, and returns automated yet contextually relevant responses. This not only speeds up response times but also frees human agents to manage more complex customer queries, thereby enhancing overall customer and agent satisfaction, as well as business efficiency and profit.

However, while low-code platforms offer significant advantages in terms of speed and ease-of-use, they come with a variety of limitations. The abstraction layers that make these platforms user-friendly can also restrict their customization. Users might find it challenging to implement highly specialized functionality or optimize performance beyond the provided templates. Moreover, reliance on third-party services means that any changes in external APIs or platform policies could impact the functionality and scalability of the deployed agent.

Another consideration is the integration depth. Although no-code tools excel at connecting a variety of applications, the orchestration of complex workflows or the handling of high-volume data may require additional custom logic. In such cases, organizations often consider hybrid approaches, combining low-code solutions with custom code, to bridge any gaps between off-the-shelf functionality and bespoke business requirements that may exist.

Overall, low-code agent development represents a compelling option for organizations aiming to quickly deploy intelligent systems with minimal overhead. It lowers the barrier to entry for AI integration and provides a practical solution for common business challenges. However, low-code platforms are opinionated. They assume you want a linear workflow, basic LLM integration, and cloud hosting.

If the goal at hand is building something like a real-time fraud detection system that cross-references 20 APIs with millisecond latency, currently, low-code is not the right approach. The likelihood of low-code meeting your needs scales inversely with the *nicheness* of the problem. If your task is generic (e.g., "answer FAQs"), lean on templates. If it is niche (e.g., "predict rare equipment failures in nuclear plants"), prepare to write code.

Hybrid Approaches

Hybrid systems leverage low code to manage routine tasks while reserving custom code for critical components. This blended strategy enables organizations to quickly prototype AI agents using low-code tools while implementing niche functionalities using custom code wherever necessary. By adopting a hybrid approach, organizations can address specific needs that off-the-shelf solutions might not fully cover, ensuring that the resulting system is both robust and adaptable.

One practical example is the development of a Sales Lead Qualification Agent. In this scenario, a low-code platform might initially be used to establish basic data flows, integrate with

Customer Relationship Management (CRM) systems, and quickly set up communication channels. Once the foundational workflows are in place, developers can embed custom Python scripts to perform advanced analytics and decision-making.

For instance, a custom module could analyze historical sales data to adjust lead scoring dynamically, incorporate machine learning models to predict lead conversion probabilities or execute complex filtering algorithms based on specific business rules. This tailored coding not only refines the agent's accuracy in qualifying leads but also integrates seamlessly with broader enterprise systems.

To achieve success with a hybrid approach, several best practices should be followed:

1. **Modular Design.** Structure your project so that low-code components and custom-code modules operate as independent yet interconnected units. This modularization ensures that each component can be updated, replaced, or scaled without impacting the overall system functionality.

2. **Clear Interface Boundaries.** Clear interfaces between the low-code and custom-coded components. Use well-documented APIs and data exchange formats to ensure smooth integration. This minimizes the risk of miscommunication between systems and reduces developer troubleshooting time.

3. **Robust Testing and Monitoring.** Implement comprehensive testing strategies that cover both the low-code workflows and the custom scripts. Continuous integration and automated testing help catch errors early. Additionally, set up monitoring tools to track performance metrics and identify potential bottlenecks or failures in real-time.

4. **Scalability Considerations.** Plan for scalability from the outset. While low-code platforms often manage basic scaling automatically, custom code should be designed with scalability in mind. Use cloud-based services and containerization where appropriate to ensure that increased load or data volume does not compromise performance.

5. **Documentation and Collaboration.** Maintain thorough documentation that details how the low-code components interact with the custom code. This practice supports future development efforts, facilitates knowledge transfer within teams, and ensures that maintenance remains manageable over time.

In summary, hybrid approaches offer a balanced solution for organizations that need rapid deployment and customization. Hybrid is not a compromise—it is strategic arbitrage. Low code's efficiency for routine tasks can be harnessed, with the time saved reinvested in developing tailored logic that sets you apart.

Full-Code Agent Development

Coding an agent from scratch offers extensive control and customization, letting developers create precise solutions for business requirements. This approach must be taken when off-the-shelf or low-code solutions simply fail to provide the necessary flexibility or performance. Python has emerged as the language of choice for many full code projects due to its extensive ecosystem, readability, and ease of integration with various AI frameworks.

Building from Scratch with Python

Developing an agent fully in code begins with setting up the environment using Python. Developers typically leverage frameworks such as Flask or FastAPI for building APIs, along with libraries like Requests for handling external API calls. The advantage of this approach is that it enables the creation of a tailored architecture where every component can be finely tuned and optimized.

Core Components of a Full-Code Agent.

A well-designed full-code agent comprises three core components: memory, reasoning, and action.

- **Memory:** Memory in an agent refers to its ability to store and recall context over interactions. This can be achieved using in-memory data structures for short-term tasks or persistent databases like SQLite, PostgreSQL, or NoSQL solutions for long-term storage. Effective memory management is crucial for applications that require context awareness, such as conversational agents or systems that track user interactions over time.

- **Reasoning:** The reasoning component is responsible for decision-making. This is where the integration of Language Learning Models (LLMs) such as OpenAI's GPT or other advanced machine learning models comes into play. Developers can use Python libraries like Hugging Face's Transformers to implement complex natural language processing tasks. Custom algorithms and logic can further refine the outputs from these models, enabling the agent to interpret inputs, process data, and generate intelligent responses.

- **Action:** Once a decision is made, the agent must act. This involves triggering responses, interacting with databases, or making external API calls. Custom code can be written to manage these operations reliably, ensuring that actions are executed in a secure and efficient manner. This component is critical in scenarios where the agent needs to modify system states, trigger workflows, or provide real-time feedback.

An example of full code development is the creation of Data Analysis Agents. In such a scenario, an organization would need to automate the process of analyzing large datasets and generating custom reports.

By developing a full code solution, developers can integrate Python libraries such as Pandas and NumPy for data manipulation alongside visualization tools like Matplotlib or Seaborn for rendering insights. The agent's memory component stores historical data and contextual information, while its reasoning component processes complex queries and patterns in the data.

Finally, the action component automates the generation and distribution of customized reports. This comprehensive setup ensures that the agent not only analyses data accurately but also adapts to evolving data patterns over time.

Advanced Features: Reflection and Planning

Beyond the core components, advanced features can elevate a full-code agent from a basic tool to a sophisticated system capable of self-improvement and strategic operation.

- **Reflection.** Reflection involves the agent's ability to evaluate its past performance and outcomes. By implementing logging and feedback loops, developers can enable the agent to assess the effectiveness of its actions and decision-making processes. This self-assessment mechanism allows for iterative improvements and adjustments in strategies, ultimately leading to a more refined and efficient system.

- **Planning.** Planning is the capability to execute multi-step tasks that require foresight and scheduling. By incorporating planning libraries or custom-developed algorithms, an agent can manage sequences of actions that consider both immediate and long-term objectives. This is particularly useful in scenarios like supply chain management or strategic business planning, where sequential decision-making and future state predictions are critical.

Full-code agent development offers the highest degree of flexibility and performance by allowing developers to build every aspect of the agent from the ground up. Although this approach requires more time and technical expertise compared to low-code alternatives, the resulting system is capable of handling complex, high-volume tasks with advanced features such as reflection and multi-step planning. For organizations with specific requirements and the resources to invest in bespoke development, full-code solutions present an ideal path to achieving a highly optimized and adaptable AI agent.

Choosing the Right Approach

CTOs and CIOs often face a critical decision: leverage low-code solutions for rapid results or invest in full-code development for long-term gains. This decision can be framed as a multi-armed bandit problem, where each choice carries trade-offs. Below is a structured approach to evaluating the best path forward.

Key Variables to Consider

1. **Problem Complexity:**

   o **Low Complexity:** Tasks like, "Sending follow-up emails after meetings," are well-suited for low-code solutions.

   o **High Complexity:** Challenges such as, "Predicting ICU patient deterioration using real-time vitals," typically require full-code development for precision and customization.

2. **Technical Debt Tolerance:**

   o Low-code solutions can introduce hidden technical debt. For example, a Shopify store relying on 50 Zapier automation may face significant risks if API changes occur.

3. **Scaling Trajectory**:

   ○ Consider whether your solution needs to manage significantly larger volumes of data or users in the future. Custom code often provides cleaner scalability for high-growth scenarios.

Conclusion: The Future where Code and No-Code Converge

Agentic AI architecture presents a spectrum of development strategies, from low-code rapid prototyping to full-code custom solutions, each with its distinct advantages. The distinction between low code and full code is becoming increasingly blurred.

Platforms such as Replit now allow for in-browser code editing, while technologies like ChatGPT can generate Python scripts from natural language prompts. In the future, a CTO might simply describe an agent in plain English, observe AI scaffold the solution, and then manually fine-tune the code to deliver the solution.

References

- https://stackoverflow.blog/2023/12/28/self-healing-code-is-the-future-of-software-development/

- https://aws.amazon.com/bedrock/

- https://cloud.google.com/vertex-ai/docs/beginner/beginners-guide

Chapter 11

Agentic AI:
Your Personalized Power-Up for a Better Life

11

Agentic AI: Your Personalized Power-Up for a Better Life

Picture this: It is 8 a.m., and your phone buzzes with a dozen unread emails. Your calendar pings with back-to-back meetings. News alerts flood your screen, social media demands your attention, and your to-do list grows faster than you can tackle it. By noon, you are drowning in tasks, yet somehow, nothing feels truly *done*. Sound familiar? In an age of endless demands and infinite information, the quest for balance often feels like a losing battle. This is where Agentic AI comes into its own. Unlike regular LLMs that wait for prompts, Agentic AI systems function as autonomous collaborators. Think of them as digital "agents" with the ability to understand, reason, and act independently within defined boundaries. These agents learn your preferences, anticipate your needs, and execute tasks without micromanagement. Imagine a personal assistant who not only schedules your meetings but negotiates timing conflicts, filters out irrelevant emails, and even drafts replies in your tone. That is the promise of Agentic AI: intelligence that works for you, not the other way around.

But what makes this technology revolutionary is not just automation—it is *agency*. By combining advanced machine learning with decision-making frameworks, agents adapt to dynamic environments, solve problems creatively, and evolve alongside their goals. Understanding how these systems operate, their strengths, limitations, and ethical implications empowers us to harness their potential responsibly. The future is not about humans versus machines; it is about humans and machines collaborating to build richer, more intentional lives. Let us explore how.

Agents as Your Personal Productivity Multipliers

Reclaim Your Time and Focus

In a world where time is the ultimate currency, Agentic AI is emerging as a game-changer. By automating drudgery, cutting through noise, and streamlining workflows, these systems do not just optimize your day—they give you back the mental space to thrive.

Automating Mundane Tasks

Consider the hours lost each week to repetitive chores: sorting emails, scheduling appointments, or updating spreadsheets. Agentic AI tackles these tasks with precision. For instance, an email management agent can prioritize messages based on urgency, draft responses to routine inquiries, and even flag critical threads for your attention. Tools like AI-powered schedulers analyze your habits to book meetings at optimal times, while data entry agents auto-populate forms and databases, reducing human error.

The benefit? Freed from the "small stuff," you regain hours for creative problem-solving, strategic thinking, or simply recharging. As Cal Newport, author of Deep Work, argues, eliminating "shallow" tasks is key to unlocking meaningful productivity. Agentic AI makes this all possible.

Intelligent Information Filtering

We live in an era of information paralysis. Agentic AI cuts through the clutter by acting as a personalized curator. Imagine a news aggregator that distills global events into concise briefs tailored to your interests or a research assistant who scours academic journals and highlights findings relevant to your project. Social media agents can mute toxic content, amplify valuable connections, and even prompt you to step away when scrolling becomes mindless. By surfacing only what matters, agents help you stay informed without drowning you in data.

Smart Assistants for Work and Life

Agentic AI's true power lies in handling complexity. Take project management: An agent could break down a multi-phase initiative into actionable steps, assign tasks to team members based on their bandwidth, and adjust deadlines dynamically as priorities shift. In your personal life, travel-planning agents compare flights, hotels, and local events to design itineraries that align with your budget and preferences. Even shopping becomes effortless with agents that track price drops, suggest eco-friendly alternatives, or automate grocery restocking.

These agents function as force multipliers, turning fragmented efforts into cohesive outcomes. As IBM's research highlights, organizations using AI-driven tools report 30-40% gains in operational efficiency, a potential that extends to individuals.

Agentic AI is not about doing more; it is about accomplishing more of what matters. By offloading routine work and amplifying focus, these systems let us reclaim our most finite resource: attention.

Agents for Personalized Experiences and Growth

Tailored to You: Agents that Understand Your Needs

In today's world, one-size-fits-all solutions rarely meet our personal needs. This is where Agentic AI truly shines by tailoring experiences and growth opportunities to our unique preferences, abilities, and goals. Imagine having an intelligent companion who not only understands your learning style but also sparks your creativity and curates entertainment just for you. Agentic AI is evolving to become a personalized guide in our educational journeys, creative endeavors, or leisure pursuits, empowering us to thrive in an ever-changing landscape.

Personalized Learning and Education

Traditional education has often followed a rigid path, leaving many students struggling to keep pace or feeling unchallenged. Enter Agentic AI: modern AI tutors and customized learning platforms that adapt in real-time to your strengths and weaknesses. These systems analyze your performance, recognize patterns in your understanding, and create learning paths that are as unique as you are.

For instance, consider an AI tutor that identifies when you are struggling to grasp a new concept. It watches you and then dynamically tailors learning content to your specific needs. The personalized AI tutor might provide new challenges, questions, or video or audio content, breaking topics into more digestible parts to help you become unstuck. With tools tailored to your unique needs, like adaptive quizzes, interactive simulations, and immediate feedback, the process of learning becomes more engaging and effective. Not only does this personalized approach accelerate skill acquisition, but it also caters to various learning styles, whether you are a visual learner, an auditory enthusiast, or someone who thrives on hands-on experience.

Moreover, agents extend beyond traditional academics. They can guide professional development by recommending tailored learning resources, creating customized training modules, and even simulating real-world scenarios for practice. In doing so, they transform the learning experience from a static classroom environment into a dynamic, lifelong process that adapts to your evolving interests and career demands. (source)

Enhanced Creativity and Inspiration

Creativity often blooms when we are free to explore and experiment, yet many of us hit a creative block or struggle to find inspiration. Agentic AI is stepping in as a virtual muse, one that not only offers ideas but also collaborates with us to overcome creative hurdles. AI writing assistants, for example, can suggest narrative arcs or dialogue options for a budding novelist, while design agents can propose fresh visual elements for artists looking for a new perspective.

Take an AI-powered music composition tool: by analyzing your preferred genres and moods, it can generate unique soundscapes that serve as both inspiration and a creative jump-start. Similarly, digital design platforms powered by AI can recommend color palettes, layout adjustments, and even entire design concepts that align with your aesthetic preferences. This kind of assistance does not replace your creative vision but rather expands the realm of possibilities, encouraging you to take creative risks and experiment with new ideas.

The collaboration between human creativity and machine intelligence can be especially powerful. When an AI agent suggests a starting point, be it a sketch, a rough draft, or a melody, you can refine and build upon that foundation. Over time, these interactions help refine your creative process, making it more efficient and less prone to stagnation. The result is a synergistic relationship where both human ingenuity and AI capabilities work in tandem, unlocking creative potentials that might otherwise remain untapped.

Agents for Entertainment and Leisure

Our leisure time is increasingly shaped by digital content, and Agentic AI is transforming how we engage with entertainment.

In an era marked by an overwhelming abundance of options, AI can help tailor your recreational experiences to suit your tastes and moods. Whether it is personalized content recommendations on streaming platforms or interactive storytelling that evolves based on your choices, AI agents are set to redefine our downtime.

Imagine an AI companion that not only suggests movies or books but curates a whole experience around them. It might organize virtual watch parties, generate themed playlists, or even provide trivia and discussion points related to your favorite shows. In the realm of interactive storytelling, AI agents can co-create narratives with you, where the storyline adapts dynamically to your input, transforming passive consumption into an engaging, participatory adventure.

Moreover, AI-driven platforms are becoming adept at identifying subtle preferences through your interactions, gradually refining recommendations so that your entertainment choices resonate more deeply with your personal tastes. This level of customization ensures that your leisure time is not only more enjoyable but also more fulfilling, as you are consistently introduced to content that reflects your evolving interests.

Agents for personalized experiences are more than mere tools–they are catalysts for growth, creativity, and enriched leisure. By tailoring educational content, igniting creative sparks, and curating our entertainment, these AI agents empower us to lead more balanced and fulfilled lives, finely tuned to our personal rhythms and ambitions.

Agents for a Healthier and More Accessible Life

Agents Caring for Your Wellbeing

Beyond enhancing productivity and personal growth, Agentic AI is poised to revolutionize how we care for our health and ensure that everyone, regardless of ability, can access the benefits of modern technology. From proactive health monitoring to smart home integrations that adapt to our physical needs, these AI agents are dedicated to creating a safer, more inclusive, and healthier environment.

Personalized Health Monitoring and Wellness

Imagine waking up to an AI agent that not only tracks your sleep patterns but also analyses them to suggest improvements for a more restorative rest. Today's health-monitoring devices, enhanced by Agentic AI, do much more than merely record data. They provide insights that guide us toward better physical and mental health. Whether it is through fitness trackers, wearable diagnostic tools, or mental health apps, these agents continuously monitor key health metrics and offer personalized recommendations.

For example, an AI-driven health assistant can monitor your daily activity levels, heart rate, and even stress indicators, alerting you to potential issues before they escalate. By comparing your current data with established health benchmarks and your own historical trends it can suggest changes in diet, exercise routines, or sleep habits. This proactive approach to health management not only helps in the early detection of issues but also empowers you to make informed lifestyle decisions that lead to long-term wellness.

Additionally, mental well-being is increasingly recognized as a crucial component of overall health. AI-powered apps now offer personalized meditation routines, cognitive behavioral therapy (CBT) exercises, and mood tracking. These digital companions can provide immediate support during stressful moments, suggest mindfulness practices tailored to your current emotional state, and even recommend professional help if needed. In this way, Agentic AI serves as a first line of defense, promoting a holistic approach to health that integrates both physical and mental care.

Agents for Accessibility and Inclusivity

One of the most exciting aspects of Agentic AI is its potential to level the playing field for individuals with disabilities. By leveraging intelligent algorithms, AI agents are breaking down traditional barriers and making technology more accessible. Whether it is through speech-to-text systems, visual recognition software, or personalized accessibility settings, these tools are empowering people to engage with the digital world more fully.

For instance, consider an AI-powered translation agent that can convert spoken language into text in real-time, enabling individuals with hearing impairments to participate seamlessly in conversations. Similarly, visually impaired users can benefit from image recognition tools that describe their surroundings, read text aloud, or even identify objects. These technologies not only enhance everyday interactions but also foster greater independence, allowing users to navigate public spaces and digital content with confidence.

Moreover, Agentic AI can customize accessibility settings based on individual needs. By learning your preferences, such as font size, contrast settings, or navigation styles, AI agents can automatically adjust interfaces to ensure optimal readability and ease of use. This level of personalization is particularly impactful in educational and professional settings, where inclusive design is paramount to ensuring that everyone has equal access to information and opportunities.

Agents for Smarter Homes and Environments

Finally, the promise of Agentic AI extends to our very living spaces. Smart home technology, when powered by advanced AI agents, transforms our environments into responsive, adaptive sanctuaries. Imagine a home that learns your routine and adjusts lighting, temperature, and even background music to create the perfect atmosphere for relaxation or productivity.

Smart home agents integrate seamlessly with a variety of Internet of Things (IoT) devices, from thermostats and security cameras to energy management systems, creating a cohesive ecosystem that prioritizes your comfort and efficiency. These agents can monitor energy consumption, optimize heating and cooling patterns, and even suggest adjustments based on weather forecasts or occupancy levels, leading to significant cost savings and a reduced environmental footprint.

Furthermore, the accessibility benefits of smart home agents cannot be overstated. For seniors or individuals with mobility challenges, voice-activated systems can control nearly every aspect of the home environment, from opening doors to adjusting blinds. This not only enhances safety but also provides a greater sense of autonomy and independence. By seamlessly integrating health monitoring, accessibility features, and energy management, these agents foster a living environment that is truly attuned to your needs.

Conclusion

In conclusion, Agentic AI represents a transformative shift that redefines every facet of our lives, from personal productivity and creative exploration to health management and inclusive living. The journey through personalized learning, tailored entertainment, and proactive well-being demonstrates that these intelligent agents can empower us to reclaim our time and focus on what truly matters.

Yet, this bright future hinges on responsible development. Emphasizing ethical practices, data privacy, and bias mitigation is crucial to ensure that AI serves as a trusted partner rather than a disruptive force. By embracing Agentic AI thoughtfully, we pave the way for a future where technology enhances our human experience and redefines what it means to lead a fulfilling life.

Ultimately, the evolution of Agentic AI invites us to reimagine our potential. With careful guidance and a commitment to ethical principles, we can harness these advancements to create a world where every individual can thrive, innovate, and enjoy a truly better life.

References:

- https://blogs.nvidia.com/blog/what-is-agentic-ai/

- https://thinkers50.com/blog/work-and-life/deep-vs-shallow-work-cal-newport/

- https://www.forbes.com/sites/bernardmarr/2024/03/29/generative-ai-is-coming-to-your-home-appliances/

- https://www.business-standard.com/organizations/news/ibm-software-sees-30-40-productivity-gains-among-developers-using-genai-124070901060_1.html

- https://training.safetyculture.com/blog/adaptive-learning-platforms/

- https://www.forbes.com/councils/forbestechcouncil/2024/11/08/ai-is-personalizing-our-entertainment-experiences-in-big-ways/

Chapter 12

The Future of Work
and Society with Agents

The Future of Work and Society with Agents

Picture a world where AI does not simply respond to queries but collaborates with us to solve problems, optimize entire industries, and even spark creative insights–all on its own. This is the promise of Agentic AI, systems that do not just follow instructions but act autonomously to achieve goals, and they represent the next evolutionary leap beyond traditional automation. These systems can reason, learn, and adapt in ways that blur the line between tool and collaborator. Yet, with this power comes profound questions: How much autonomy should we grant machines? How do we ensure they align with human values? And what happens when they outperform us in domains we once considered uniquely human?

To see agentic AI at work, consider UPS and its ORION system. UPS implemented ORION (On-Road Integrated

Optimization and Navigation), an AI-driven route optimization system that processes real-time data to determine the most efficient delivery routes. Since its deployment, UPS ORION has been reported as saving millions of miles annually, reducing fuel consumption, and cutting operational costs significantly, all while improving delivery efficiency.

Agentic AI is already here, making its mark in logistics, scientific research, and beyond, but this transformative power also brings new challenges. But as we embrace their potential, we must also be careful: the future of AI is not just about what machines **can** do. It is about what we, as a society, **choose** to let them do.

What Makes Agentic AI "Agentic"? Key Capabilities

At the heart of agentic AI lies a set of distinctive capabilities that separate it from traditional automation. First and foremost is goal-oriented behavior. Unlike conventional systems that execute tasks in a linear, predetermined manner, agentic AI is built to achieve specific outcomes. Take the ORION system: its objective is not just to follow a static route but to minimize fuel consumption while ensuring timely deliveries. Every decision made by the system is aligned with this ultimate goal, ensuring that the company's strategic targets are met consistently.

Equally crucial is autonomous decision-making. In an ever-changing environment, waiting for human intervention is impractical. Agentic AI systems are engineered to analyze real-time data and make independent choices. For example, if an unexpected roadblock appears, the system can instantly recalibrate, selecting an alternate route without pausing operations. This capability not only boosts efficiency but also enhances responsiveness to unforeseen challenges.

Another cornerstone is learning and adaptation. Agentic AI does not remain static; it evolves through continuous exposure to new data. Using machine learning techniques, these systems refine their strategies over time, much like a seasoned driver who adjusts to road conditions based on past experiences. This adaptability means that the system grows more effective and resilient with every decision, transforming raw data into actionable intelligence.

Complex reasoning further elevates agentic AI. Beyond simple cause-and-effect scenarios, these systems can evaluate multifaceted situations involving numerous interdependent variables. In a manufacturing setting, for instance, an agentic AI might analyze production schedules, machine performance, and supply chain logistics to optimize the entire operation. This level of reasoning ensures that decisions are not only quick but also deeply informed by the broader context.

Finally, the capability for interaction and collaboration distinguishes agentic AI as a true partner in innovation. These systems are designed to communicate seamlessly with both other AI agents and human teams. In environments like smart factories or integrated energy grids, agentic AI units can coordinate their actions, share insights, and work in tandem with human experts to tackle complex challenges. This collaborative approach ensures that while the technology drives efficiency, human oversight and creativity remain integral to the decision-making process.

Together, these key capabilities transform agentic AI from a mere tool into a dynamic, strategic one that anticipates challenges, learns from experience, and works collaboratively to push the boundaries of what is possible.

Industry by Industry: Agentic AI Use Cases

Agentic AI is rapidly transcending its experimental origins to deliver tangible business value across a spectrum of industries. By leveraging goal-oriented behavior, autonomous decision-making, adaptive learning, complex reasoning, and collaborative interaction, these systems are not only streamlining operations but also enabling companies to reimagine entire business models. Below, we explore several key sectors where agentic AI is making a profound impact.

Manufacturing: Redefining Efficiency on the Factory Floor

In modern manufacturing, agentic AI is revolutionizing how factories operate. Consider Siemens' initiatives in smart manufacturing, where integrated AI systems autonomously schedule production, manage inventory and optimize energy consumption. These systems analyze sensor data from machinery and production lines in real time, predicting equipment failures before they occur and adjusting workflows on the fly.

This approach minimizes downtime and waste while ensuring optimal use of resources. For instance, Siemens' smart factory solutions have been instrumental in achieving significant efficiency gains, underscoring how agentic AI shifts the focus from reactive maintenance to proactive management.

By continuously learning from operational data, these AI agents improve their decision-making processes over time. This not only reduces the need for constant human oversight but also allows the system to manage increasingly complex production scenarios. The result is a dynamic manufacturing environment where both speed and precision are enhanced, driving down costs and boosting overall productivity.

Agriculture: Precision Farming in the Age of AI

The agricultural sector, long reliant on traditional practices, is experiencing a technological renaissance powered by agentic AI. One prominent example is the integration of AI-driven systems by companies such as John Deere, which acquired Blue River Technology. Their precision agriculture platforms use advanced sensors, drones, and imaging technology to monitor crop health, soil conditions, and weather patterns. By processing this data autonomously, the system can adjust irrigation, fertilization, and pesticide application in real-time.

This technology ensures that crops receive the precise amount of water and nutrients they need, reducing waste and maximizing yields. John Deere's approach, highlighted in their Precision Agriculture solutions, demonstrates how agentic AI transforms traditional farming into a data-driven, efficient operation. By autonomously managing complex variables, these systems help farmers make more informed decisions, paving the way for sustainable agriculture practices that can better withstand environmental challenges.

Energy Management: Balancing Grids in Real-Time

In the energy sector, the challenge of integrating renewable sources with traditional power generation is both complex and critical. Agentic AI is playing a pivotal role in modernizing energy management through the creation of smart grids. Companies like NextEra Energy and GE Grid Solutions are at the forefront, employing AI systems that continuously monitor energy demand and supply, predict fluctuations, and autonomously adjust distribution strategies to maintain grid stability.

These AI-driven systems are designed to balance the intermittent nature of renewable energy sources, such as solar and wind, with conventional power supplies. For example, by predicting a surge in energy demand or a drop in renewable output, the system can seamlessly integrate stored energy or adjust loads to avoid blackouts. This dynamic management not only enhances reliability but also optimizes energy usage, reducing waste and lowering operational costs.

Research and Development: Accelerating Innovation in Science

Agentic AI is also making waves in research and development (R&D), particularly in fields where the volume of data and complexity of experimentation are skyrocketing. In pharmaceutical research, for instance, companies like IBM have leveraged AI systems, such as IBM Watson, to autonomously design experiments, analyze vast datasets, and even generate novel hypotheses for drug discovery. These systems can screen millions of compounds in a fraction of the time required by traditional methods, identifying promising candidates with remarkable efficiency.

By integrating continuous learning and complex reasoning, agentic AI in R&D not only speeds up the discovery process but also reduces costs and mitigates risks associated with drug development. The success of IBM Watson Health, detailed in IBM's Watson Health initiatives, exemplifies how these systems serve as a catalyst for scientific innovation, transforming data into actionable insights that push the boundaries of medical research and beyond.

Creative Industries: Empowering Artistic Innovation

While the term "agentic AI" might conjure images of industrial robots and automated decision-making, its influence extends into the creative industries as well. In realms such as music, film, and visual arts, agentic AI is emerging as a valuable collaborator rather than a mere tool. Projects like The Next Rembrandt showcase how AI can analyze historical art data to create new works that echo the genius of past masters. Here, the system autonomously learns from thousands of paintings and then synthesizes its understanding into a new piece that is both innovative and respectful of tradition.

Beyond visual arts, AI platforms are increasingly assisting in content creation across various media. For example, companies are deploying AI tools to help musicians compose music, generate scripts for filmmakers, and even create personalized entertainment experiences. These systems operate not as replacements for human creativity but as extensions of it, offering new perspectives and sparking collaboration between humans and machines. The ability of agentic AI to engage in complex reasoning and adapt to creative inputs makes it an invaluable partner in the quest for novel artistic expressions.

The Societal Implications of Agentic AI

Agentic AI's societal implications are profound and multifaceted. Economically, it is reshaping job markets by shifting demand toward data-driven, strategic roles while automating routine tasks, which makes it imperative for industries to invest in reskilling programs to help workers transition into AI-enhanced roles. At the same time, ethical and legal challenges such as bias, transparency, and accountability in AI decision-making are prompting the development of robust governance frameworks, as exemplified by initiatives like the EU AI Act.

Socially, as AI becomes an integral part of daily life, our notions of creativity, intelligence, and human uniqueness are evolving, underscoring the critical need to maintain human agency in an increasingly automated world.

Additionally, with AI systems managing vast amounts of sensitive data, issues of privacy, security, and data sovereignty have come to the forefront, requiring organizations to prioritize encryption, transparency, and adherence to global data regulations. Finally, while developed economies rapidly advance with AI technologies, developing nations risk being left behind, highlighting the urgency for policies that ensure AI accessibility, education, and equitable distribution of its benefits.

Addressing the Sceptics: Navigating Concerns and Misconceptions

Artificial Intelligence (AI) is often met with skepticism, with concerns ranging from overhyped expectations to fears of job displacement and uncontrollable risks. However, beyond speculation, AI is already delivering tangible benefits across industries, from revolutionizing scientific breakthroughs to optimizing business operations. While misconceptions persist, real-world applications demonstrate that AI is neither an abstract future concept nor an existential threat but a transformative tool shaping modern society.

This section explores common doubts about AI and provides a balanced perspective on its challenges and opportunities, illustrating how agentic AI is driving progress while being actively managed through regulation, innovation, and responsible deployment.

AI is just hype

While overinflated expectations exist, agentic AI has already demonstrated measurable impact. Consider DeepMind's AlphaFold, which solved a 50-year-old challenge in biology by predicting protein structures with atomic precision, accelerating drug discovery and materials science. Similarly, Siemens employs digital twin technology and predictive analytics to optimize performance, enhance efficiency, and reduce emissions. These are not speculative demos; they are deployed tools actively reshaping industries.

AI will steal all our jobs

History shows technology creates more roles than it destroys, but transitions matter. IBM's "skills-first" approach exemplifies proactive adaptation: they've retrained over 400,000 employees in AI and cloud skills since 2014, shifting roles toward higher-value tasks like managing AI-driven supply chains. Agentic AI won't replace radiologists, but systems like Aidoc (which flags critical anomalies in medical scans 24/7) let clinicians focus on complex diagnoses and patient care.

AI is uncontrollable and dangerous

Risks exist, but frameworks are emerging. DeepMind's SAFE is an AI tool to fact-check LLMs. The EU's AI Act mandates strict oversight for high-risk applications, such as autonomous vehicles. Crucially, agentic AI today operates within bounded domains, unlike sci-fi AGI. For example, Boston Dynamics' Spot robot navigates industrial inspections autonomously but follows strict safety protocols and human override commands.

AI is too complex and expensive

Cloud platforms like AWS SageMaker and Google Vertex AI now offer pre-trained agentic models for tasks like demand forecasting or fraud detection, slashing development costs. Startups like Olive automate healthcare billing using no-code AI tools, proving even non-technical teams can deploy solutions. The ROI speaks for itself: Walmart's AI-powered inventory management reduced out-of-stock items by 20%, translating to billions in recovered revenue.

A balanced approach to AI recognizes both the risks and the progress being made.

Conclusion: Embracing the Agentic Future with Confidence and Foresight

In conclusion, the rise of agentic AI marks not merely an incremental technological improvement but a profound transformation in how organizations operate and innovate. By transitioning from passive automation to systems that think, learn, and adapt autonomously, industries are experiencing dramatic shifts in efficiency and strategic capability. The real-world successes of companies like Siemens and John Deere vividly illustrate that this is no distant science fiction. Agentic AI is already redefining logistics, manufacturing, agriculture, energy management, research, and the creative industries.

For CTOs and industry leaders, the imperative is clear: embrace these technologies with both ambition and caution. A measured and phased approach, starting with pilot projects to build expertise and strengthen human-AI collaboration, will help minimize risks. Equally critical is the commitment to ethical oversight, ensuring that as our AI systems grow ever more capable, they do so in a manner that upholds and enhances our human values.

The agentic revolution invites us to reimagine the future of work and innovation. With thoughtful strategy and responsible governance, we can harness these intelligent systems to elevate human creativity, solve complex challenges, and create a more resilient, dynamic world. Embrace the future with confidence and foresight. The journey toward a truly autonomous era begins now.

References:

- https://www.dronedeploy.com/blog/bowles-farm-agriculture

- https://bostondynamics.com/products/spot/

- https://techxplore.com/news/2024-03-deepmind-safe-ai-based-app.html

- https://arxiv.org/abs/2403.18802

- https://www.aidoc.com/

- https://www.sw.siemens.com/en-US/technology/digital-twin/

- https://cloud.google.com/vertex-ai/docs/start/introduction-unified-platform

Conclusion

The Evolution of AI: From Prediction to Agency

The landscape of artificial intelligence (AI) has undergone significant transformation, evolving through three distinct waves. The first wave, predictive AI, focused on analyzing historical data to forecast trends and support data-driven decision-making. It enabled organizations to predict outcomes but lacked the capability for creativity or autonomous action.

The second wave, generative AI, introduced the ability to create content, allowing systems to engage in human-like conversations, generate images, and produce written content. Generative AI captivated industries with its creativity and versatility but remained fundamentally reactive to human input.

Now, we stand on the cusp of the third wave: Agentic AI. Unlike its predecessors, Agentic AI is not just about automation; it is about endowing machines with agency. It represents a fundamental shift in capability, enabling AI systems to act autonomously, make decisions, and adapt dynamically to complex environments.

The convergence of advanced machine learning, cloud computing, and large language models (LLMs) drives this evolution forward. Together, these advancements empower AI systems to not only understand human intent but also to independently execute tasks and collaborate with other agents to achieve goals.

The third wave of AI ushers in a new era of possibilities, where machines can autonomously execute tasks, collaborate with other agents, and adapt to dynamic environments. While the opportunities are immense, so are the challenges. Organizations must navigate the complexities of trust, workforce transformation, and ethical deployment to realize the full potential of Agentic AI.

The time to prepare for this transformation is now. By embracing responsible adoption and fostering collaboration between humans and AI, organizations can harness the power of Agentic AI to drive innovation, efficiency, and growth. The future of work is here, and it is powered by agents.

The Future of Work Is Digital

That said, we live in a time of extraordinary promise. The future of work and digital labor has always faced disruption. For example, there are far fewer saddlers today than there are software engineers. But the pace at which organizations, their leaders and workers face disruption is accelerating like never before. The value by which we were once measured, our ability to collect, synthesize and repeat learning, is now being removed thanks to generative AI and large language models' ability to do exactly that.

Agentic labor markets and models are a feature, not of the future but of today. Gone are the days when there was an app for that - now there is, or soon will be, an agent for that.

Whilst many will claim that Agentic AI is a revolution, I consider it a continued, and accelerating evolution of workplaces that has been wrought by technology over the ages. That said, this evolution of digital workers, agents, or Agentic AI, will have a much more dramatic impact on work and society than any AI we have seen to date.

The fact that Agentic AI does not just execute tasks, it thinks, plans, actions, reasons, and adapts. Agents collaborate with each other and people across computer systems and networks, reshaping organizations and transforming how work gets done.

In many instances, AI agents will enhance workforce capabilities by autonomously problem-solving and completing complex tasks. Yet increasingly, rather than assisting humans, as agents get smarter, they will increasingly replace human labor.

This will pose challenges for workers and leaders everywhere. The challenge for leaders is in reimagining how their organizations operate in an Agentic age.

This change has huge implications for workers, governments, educators, and workers everywhere. It is for you to lead the change, not be a victim of it. I wish you every success in your Agentic AI journey.

Kieran Gilmurray

Glossary of Terms

Artificial Intelligence (AI) - Artificial Intelligence is the development of computer software to perform tasks normally requiring human intelligence, such as visual perception, speech recognition, decision-making, and translation between languages. AI is not new. The term 'artificial intelligence' was coined in 1956 during the Dartmouth workshop, a gathering of scientists intent on exploring the potential of computing to emulate human reasoning. Since then, there have been recurring waves of progress and excitement, known as 'AI summers,' followed by periods of waning interest and investment, referred to as 'AI winters.'

Artificial General Intelligence (AGI): Artificial General Intelligence refers to highly autonomous systems that possess the ability to understand, learn, and apply intelligence across a wide range of tasks at a human-like level. Unlike narrow AI, which is designed for specific tasks such as image recognition or language translation, AGI can reason, adapt, and perform any intellectual task that a human can. The concept of AGI has been a long-standing goal in AI research, with origins dating back to the early discussions of machine intelligence. While considerable progress has been made in artificial intelligence, AGI remains largely theoretical, with ongoing debates about its feasibility, potential impact, and ethical implications.

Agentic AI - Agentic AI, also known as 'agents' or 'autonomous agents, ' refers to autonomous AI systems that can make decisions and perform actions with minimal human intervention. These agents can understand their environment, identifying the set of tools and functions at their disposal, and using those to take actions to achieve their objectives.

Agent-based systems use Foundation Models (primarily LLMs) to match their capabilities with their objectives. For example, an order processing system may have multiple agents autonomously capturing pricing and market-related data. When a request for an order is raised, the agentic system may use those prices or, seeing that they haven't been updated recently, may use another agent to retrieve the latest price available. This all happens automatically in the background because the system knows which agents can perform each task.

These systems provide a simpler way to build powerful AI-driven solutions by focusing on the capabilities of each agent and letting the AI model itself figure out the best way to achieve the system's objectives. The high level of abstraction involved in this technology makes it easier to create more efficient and effective systems that take full advantage of AI.

BIAS - Machine learning systems are described as "biased" when their decisions are determined as prejudiced or discriminatory. AI-augmented sentencing software has been found to recommend higher prison sentences for Black offenders compared to white ones, even for equal crimes. And some facial recognition software works better for white faces than black ones. These failures often happen because the data those systems were trained on reflects social inequities.

Chain-of-thought (CoT). Chain-of-thought reasoning is an AI prompting technique that enhances the problem-solving capabilities of large language models (LLMs) by guiding them to break down complex tasks into a series of logical steps12. This approach mimics human reasoning processes, allowing AI models to "think out loud" and articulate their thought process step-by-step before arriving at a final answer.

Chatbots - is a software application designed to simulate conversations with human users. These bots use a combination of pre-programmed rules and, in more advanced versions, artificial intelligence (AI) techniques like natural language processing (NLP) to understand and respond to user inputs in a natural, conversational manner. They can be used for a variety of purposes, including customer service, information acquisition, and entertainment.

Computer Vision (CV) - is a field of AI and machine learning that enables computers to interpret, analyze, and understand visual information (images and videos) to perform tasks such as object recognition, facial recognition, and scene understanding. Computer Vision systems are designed to make image data understandable and interpretable so that it can be consumed and evaluated. CV uses algorithms to break down images into pixels and process the pixels to detect edges, shapes, and colors. The system then uses this information to recognize objects, people, or scenes - similarly to how our brains process visual information - allowing computers to identify the content of images.

Foundation Models - are large-scale, general-purpose artificial intelligence models that serve as the underlying architecture for a variety of more specialized applications. Models, such as GPT-4, are trained on vast datasets and are capable of understanding and generating human-like text, making them highly versatile for various AI tasks. Their size and complexity mean that they require significant computational resources to train and are usually only available to large organizations.

Generative AI is the field of artificial intelligence that focuses on creating new content based on existing data. It is a subset of AI capable of generating text, images, audio, video, or other forms of output by using probabilistic models trained across various domains. Generative AI learns from enormous amounts of specially curated training data to discern and replicate complex patterns and structures. The output of generative AI models mimics the characteristics learned from the training data, enabling a range of novel applications. These include personalized content generation, advanced analysis and evaluation, and aiding creative processes. For a ChatBot or CRM system, generative AI can be used to create a range of helpful outputs, from writing personalized marketing content to generating synthetic data to test new features or strategies.

Examples of publicly accessible generative AI tools are ChatGPT, Claude, Gemini, and Dall-E. Generative AI is also becoming increasingly integrated into mainstream products. Examples include the Adobe Photoshop Generative Fill tool, AWS ChatOps Chatbot, Microsoft 365 Copilot, and Google Duet AI.

Hallucination - is a significant shortcoming in large language models (LLMs) and their derivative chatbots, characterized by their propensity to generate false information. Tools like Microsoft's Bing, Google's Bard, or ChatGPT, for instance, have been known to fabricate non-existent articles as references to make confident but incorrect statements.

Large Language Models (LLMs) - are at the forefront of recent AI advancements. Notable examples include OpenAI's GPT-4 and Google's BERT. These are massive artificial intelligence systems trained on extensive amounts of human language, primarily sourced from books and the internet. They analyze and learn from the patterns of words in these datasets, becoming adept at mimicking human language.

Machine Learning (ML) - Machine Learning is considered a subset of artificial intelligence (AI). Machine learning uses computer algorithms to identify patterns within data. It is the branch of AI that learns from data. Those patterns are then used to create a data model that can make predictions. With increased data and experience, the results of machine learning become more accurate - much like how humans improve with more practice.

Neural networks - are a pivotal group of algorithms in machine learning, designed to emulate the structure of the human brain. They consist of nodes, like neurons in the brain, that perform calculations on data flowing through the connections between them. These networks are characterized by their inputs (such as training data) and outputs (like predictions or classifications).

Prompt engineering - is a process in the field of artificial intelligence (AI) and natural language processing (NLP) where careful design and formulation of input queries or prompts are used to elicit desired responses from AI models. It involves crafting the instructions or questions provided to the AI system in a way that maximizes the likelihood of obtaining accurate and relevant outputs.

RAG - Retrieval-augmented generation (RAG) is a technique for refining generative AI models' precision, accuracy, and dependability by integrating information sourced from authoritative repositories. To grasp its essence, envision RAG as a legal researcher, gathering crucial facts and information from trusted legal repositories to enhance the accuracy and reliability of generative AI models, much like how a legal researcher strengthens the legal case strategy with solid legal foundations.

Super General Intelligence (SGI): Super General Intelligence refers to a hypothetical form of AI that surpasses human intelligence in virtually all aspects, including creativity, problem-solving, and emotional intelligence. Unlike Artificial General Intelligence (AGI), which matches human cognitive abilities, SGI would exceed human capabilities in every field, making it vastly more powerful. The concept of SGI is often associated with discussions about the future of AI, existential risks, and the potential for machines to independently drive scientific discovery, innovation, and societal transformation. While SGI remains purely theoretical, its potential implications, both positive and negative, are the subject of intense debate among researchers, ethicists, and policymakers.

Speech recognition - SR is a field of machine learning dedicated to processing speech. It includes both systems that convert speech into text (STT) and new speech-to-speech (S2S) systems. Computers interpret information through numbers, making the key challenge in Speech Recognition (SR) the conversion of spoken language into numerical data without losing meaning or context. To achieve this, SR models first transform audio into spectrograms–visual representations of sound frequencies over time. Deep learning (DL) models then analyze these spectrograms to identify individual sounds, words, or sentences. In Speech-to-Text (STT) systems, this process produces written text from spoken input. In Speech-to-Speech (S2S) translation, a language model further processes the recognized text to generate a translation, which is then converted back into speech in the target language.

Turing Test - The Turing Test, named after British mathematician and computer scientist Alan Turing, is a test of a machine's ability to exhibit intelligent behavior equivalent to, or indistinguishable from, that of a human. It serves as a benchmark for evaluating the "human-like" qualities of artificial intelligence.

www.ingramcontent.com/pod-product-compliance
Lightning Source LLC
Chambersburg PA
CBHW041306210326
41599CB00003B/3